Discovering
and
South Devon

Other Titles in this Series

Coghill: Discovering the Water of Leith
Crumley: Discovering the Pentland Hills
Freethy: Discovering Cheshire
Freethy: Discovering Coastal Lancashire
Freethy: Discovering Coastal Yorkshire
Freethy: Discovering Cumbria
Freethy: Discovering Exmoor and North Devon
Freethy: Discovering Inland Lancashire
Freethy: Discovering Inland Yorkshire
Freethy: Discovering Northumberland
Freethy: Discovering the Pennines
Freethy: Discovering the Yorkshire Dales
Gemmell: Discovering Arran
Green: Discovering Hadrian's Wall
Henderson: Discovering Angus & the Mearns
Hendrie: Discovering West Lothian
Lamont-Brown: Discovering Fife
Maclean: Discovering Inverness-shire
Macleod: Discovering Galloway
Macleod: Discovering the River Clyde
Murray: Discovering Dumfriesshire
Orr: Discovering Argyll, Mull and Iona
Shaw Grant: Discovering Lewis and Harris
Simpson: Discovering Banff, Moray and Nairn
Smith: Discovering Aberdeenshire
Spence: Discovering the Borders I
Strawhorn and Andrew: Discovering Ayrshire
Thompson: Discovering Speyside
I. & K. Whyte: Discovering East Lothian
Willis: Discovering the Black Isle
Withers: Discovering the Cotswolds

Discovering Dartmoor and South Devon

RON & MARLENE FREETHY

JOHN DONALD PUBLISHERS LTD
EDINBURGH

© Ron and Marlene Freethy 1992

All rights reserved. No part of this publication may be reproduced in any form or by any means without the prior permission of the publishers,
John Donald Publishers Ltd,
138 St Stephen Street, Edinburgh EH3 5AA.

ISBN 0 85976 364 1

This book is dedicated to Wilf and Minnie Jaques who first introduced the authors to the area.

British Library Cataloguing in Publication Data
A catalogue record for this book is available from the British Library.

Phototypeset by The Midlands Book Typesetting Company, Loughborough.
Printed & bound in Great Britain by Bath Press, Bath.

Introduction and Acknowledgements

More than 30 years ago, we spent our honeymoon on the East Devon coast and looked in vain for a simple guide book to cover both the history and natural history of the area. We failed to find it and after many years of writing similar guides to other areas, our publisher kindly allowed us to turn our attention to South East Devon and Dartmoor.

The River Exe rises on Exmoor, flows down to Exeter and beyond this city to Exmouth and the sea. Whilst writing *Discovering Exmoor and North Devon* we realised that Exeter was also the gateway to Dartmoor and the coast and so the seed of the present book was sown.

Typical of Dartmoor are its ponies, massive granite tors, old mills driven by fast moving streams, thatched buildings, prehistoric settlements, graceful bridges, ancient crosses and lovely churches, solid castles and a coastline typified by quaint harbours, shingle beaches and towering cliffs.

The production of any book of discovery depends upon help from many people including the ever-patient staff of Tourist Information Centres and the custodians of museums and beauty spots. We are particularly grateful to Gary Emerson based at Morwellham Quay who typified the helpful and friendly attitude. We also thank the staff of the National Shire Horse Museum at Yealverton and the Miniature Pony Farm at Moretonhampstead, the City of Plymouth Marketing Bureau and Mr Philip Willoughby for allowing us access to his archive photographs. We also thank the staff of the Primrose Line Steam Railway at Buckfastleigh, the staff of the Exeter Maritime Museum and Desna Greenhow of Otterton Mill. Even the National Park has got into the friendly and humerous atmosphere by asking those who motor over Dartmoor to "Drive with Moor Care!" Those visiting Dartmoor for the first time should take notice of the colour coded route signs which translate as follows:–

Most vehicles – signed BLACK

'Medium' vehicles – no caravans – signed BLUE
Cars and Small Vehicles only – signed BROWN

During the completion of the final draft of this book we needed a quiet base from which to drive around and check for errors and omissions. This we found in a cosy cottage attached to Budleigh Farm at Moretonhampstead where Mr and Mrs Harvey made us so welcome that our work was made much easier.

Serious students of Dartmoor's history will find nothing new in this book – indeed it is not aimed at them who have a vast library of material already available. This is meant to help those who wish to discover Dartmoor and South Devon perhaps for the first time. We hope that this book will make their explorations easier.

Contents

	Page
Introduction and Acknowledgements	v
1. Geology, History and Natural History	1
2. Around Exeter	11
3. Around Dartmoor	26
4. Inside Dartmoor	57
5. South Hams	80
6. East Devon	108
7. The English Riviera	141
8. Around Plymouth	160
Further Reading	173
Index	174

Location Map

CHAPTER 1

Geology, History and Natural History

Devon is well known to every geologist throughout the world, even those who have never heard of the English County system. A look at the Geological time chart reveals the importance of the ancient rocks of Devon in the scheme of things. This can be summarised in tabular form.

Geological Time Chart
(Years distant (m = million)

Cenozoic Era
- Quaternary Period — Holocene — 1m
- — Pleistocene — 2m
- Tertiary Period — Pliocene — 7m
- — Miocene — 26m
- — Oligocene — 38m
- — Eocene — 54m
- — Palaeocene — 70m

Mesozoic Era
- Cretaceous Period — 135m
- Upper Jurassic Period — 150m
- Lower Jurassic Period — 195m
- Triassic Period — 225m

Palaeozoic Era
- Permian Period — 280m
- Carboniferous Period — 345m
- [DEVONIAN Period] — 410m
- Silurian Period — 440m
- Ordovician Period — 530m
- Cambrian Period — 570m

Pre Cambrian Era — 2800m

Thus in Devon are found some of the most ancient rocks in the world and accounts for the fact that Dartmoor is something of a Mecca for geologists. Around 500 million years ago the area of land we now call Devon did not exist, but the whole area was a huge shallow sea, to the north of which was situated a massive continent. This was slowly but surely grinding its way south and pushing up huge mountain ranges in front of it; compared to some of these giants Everest would have been a dwarf! Although much of what is now the British Isles was affected by this mountain building, the Devon sea was left almost untouched although it must have suffered great turbulence as mighty rivers tumbled down from the soaring uplands. These obviously brought down vast quantities of mud and sand. The mud being finer, was carried further out to the sea where it eventually settled out in layers. As the sea later evaporated the water was squeezed out from between the layers to produce a type of rock known as shale, whilst the coarser sands were squeezed into sandstone. Some of these sandstones contain a great deal of iron and thus Devonian redstone is the typical rock of the county, especially on the coast.

Gradually over many millions of years the mighty mountains of the North were eroded by the weather to produce the small peaks and even the plains which we find today. As these areas became reduced in height, the once torrential rivers became gentle meanders and only the very finest particles of mud were carried out to sea. Although much of the gradually shallowing Devonian Sea was muddy there were areas of crystal clear waters and here developed a sort of British Barrier Reef, one of the most impressive stretches being between Torquay and Plymouth. The remnants of these reefs are seen in the grey limestone cliffs which typify the South Devon coastline and on which grow many fascinating plants. At this time the area we now know as Dartmoor was probably an island.

Whilst all this activity was going on more or less on the surface, all was turmoil below and volcanic activity continued over millions of years. Lava blasted out from underwater volcanoes and smothered the coral, which recovered only to be smothered again. This process which continued over millions of years produced a many decked sandwich of limestone and lava.

This was the situation some 300 million years ago, after which the sea became gradually more shallow and then changed into a swamp dominated by huge ferns. When these were smothered by mud, during fluctuating sea levels, a type of coal known in Devon as calm was produced. These measures were never thick enough to be worth mining commercially. For the next 50 million years or so the movement of continents squeezed what was left of the seas almost dry and upwellings from the molten crust beneath had an equally dramatic effect. Tremendous heat and pressure converted the shales into slates and molten rock which solidified eventually into granite and was squeezed through cracks in the crust. Whilst it was molten the granite melted all the other rocks with which it came in contact. Around 300 million years ago huge masses of molten rock were pushed up beneath what is now Devon and Cornwall, and these gradually cooled to produce the typical granite. As this rose it created a molten cocktail of chemicals which themselves solidified to produce the rich mineral deposits of arsenic, zinc, lead, copper, iron, silver, tungsten and, of course, tin. Any water which fell during the tropical rain storms of the period reached the hot granite and caused it to fracture, thus producing the china clay which has been so much a part of the recent economy of the area. In Devon the major deposits are around Shaugh Prior near Plymouth.

Over the last 60 million years, the granite has been weathered to reduce the height of the hills and to expose the masses of still resistant granite which form the Dartmoor Tors.

When we were compiling our book *Discovering Exmoor and North Devon* we were also planning *Dartmoor and South Devon* and were struck by the contrast. Why should Dartmoor have civilisations which built structures in stone whilst these were missing from Exmoor? The answer is simple – the exposed granite of Dartmoor was easily quarried and some rock fractured by the action of ice and rain produced ready-to-use stone. Dartmoor was one of the most settled areas of early Britain and the natural stone was the main reason for this. Before leaving the geology of Dartmoor a brief explanation of how the tors are thought to have been formed should be given. In 1962 Palmer and Neilson suggested that tors were formed by an upthrusting of granite which were then left in splendid isolation as the softer rocks surrounding them were eroded by frost and centuries of rain and perhaps even wind. Earlier, in 1955, Linton suggested a two-stage process. Firstly weathering had its effect, but this was followed by a period in which so-called core stones exposed by weathering tumbled inwards

The Dartmoor Tors are unique to the area. This photograph shows Brent Tor.

to produce a pile of litter around the tor. Not being experts on this or any other geological feature, we do, however, wonder if the truth might be found by combining both theories.

Obviously the soil of an area is determined by a combination of bedrock plus some input from climate, slope, natural vegetation and also the effect of human activity. Any account of Dartmoor will involve these factors, whilst on the South Devon coast another important factor is involved, and that is material carried from the uplands by rivers. These alluvial soils tend to be richer in minerals and therefore more fertile.

We now turn to the effect of human activity on the physical environment and then we will consider the fauna and flora of the area. Over most of Britain the Ice Ages meant that human settlement was impossible but Devon, although it must

A Christian preaching cross at the roadside near Princetown and overlooking the pre-historic settlement of Grimspound.

have been pretty chilly, was below the ice-line. Kent's Cavern at Torquay is set in a limestone area in which archeologists have discovered the remains of mammoth, woolly rhinoceros, hippopotamus, bear and hyena. Early human settlers must also have been in search of caves which were at a premium – a sort of prehistoric housing crisis. As the climate improved colonisation took place from the continent which until sea levels rose was connected to Britain by a land bridge. There were other inhabited limestone caves at Torbay, Yealmpton, Cattedown, Stonehouse and Oreston but there is no evidence that early people ever settled permanently on Dartmoor, although they may well have searched for game among the tree cover which in those days would have been substantial.

The badger is one of the animals inhabiting the ancient caves on and around Dartmoor which has survived to the present day.

The most common trees in those days were oak, ash, beech and elm which not only dominated the valley bottoms, but also reached the summit of even the highest of the tors around or slightly above the 2000 foot (609 metre) contour. Palaeobotanists have been able to date the dominance of these species with accuracy because each has its own uniquely shaped pollen grains which are so tough that they are preserved in the peat which is short of oxygen. Pollen is also light enough to be carried by the wind.

The earliest evidence of human activity on the uplands are megalithic tombs which were communal burial chambers built during the Neolithic period. This was also known as the New Stone Age and which peaked about 3,500 BC. The settlers came from the area between Low Countries in the north to what is now Spain and Portugal in the south. The best example of these burial chambers is found at South Brent where there is a cairn around 130 feet (39.6 metres) long. Many examples of Neolithic flintwork have been found on Dartmoor including leaf-shaped arrowheads, with some in the north of the area well away from the main settlements. This suggests the probability of temporary hunting settlements used during the summer.

Geology, History and Natural History

Anyone trying to cross the moor by road will know that the Dartmoor pony truly is wild.

The New Stone Age was followed by the Bronze Age at which time communal burials were replaced by individual tombs. The stone circles also date from this period. There are at least twelve of these rings whose diameters range from 60 to 110 feet (18.3 to 33.5 metres). As the Bronze Age progressed, the settlers penetrated further and further onto the moor and established settlements called pounds. These were circles of huts protected by a stone wall which gave the farming community some protection from their enemies and from wild animals. By far the best example is at Grimspound.

The Bronze Age settlers had the technology to fell the trees, but not the agricultural know-how to maintain the fertility of the soil and as the ground became impoverished they simply felled more woodland. Only three remnants of the ancient Dartmoor forests remain at Piles Copse, Black Tor Beare and the famous Wistman's Wood arguably the most studied arboreal environment in Britain.

Around 500 BC with the climate becoming gradually harsher, Iron Age settlers landed around Torbay and worked their

The ancient woodlands of Dartmoor still have clumps of wild daffodils thriving in the undergrowth.

way inland and either conquered or merged with the earlier and probably more lightly armed Bronze Age people. The newcomers preferred to settle on the lowland areas whilst building large forts on the hill tops which provided panoramic views and thus warning of impending danger. There is an example of a relatively low-lying fort at Berry Head and a fine upland structure at Prestonbury overlooking the Teign valley. There were many iron-age tribes in the area we now call Dartmoor and South Devon with the main group being named Dumnouii from which the county takes its name.

When the Romans came to Britain their influence was slow to push both northwards and westwards and they did not penetrate permanently beyond Exeter. Thus their erosive effect on the established Devon settlements was minimal. The South

Devon coastline has many bays which were suitable landing points for small boats and some intrusions were made from the continent by tribes hostile to Rome. The Imperial reaction was predictable and striking out from Exeter roads were built to the Tamar to the west, Totnes in the south and beyond this to the coast. Protective forts were built at strategic points rather than at regular intervals. Between the Romans leaving and the Normans arriving there is no evidence of Dartmoor being used for anything other than for grazing farm stock but in the 12th century the importance of its rich minerals, especially tin, was realised. Early mining techniques were only capable of removing deposits close to the surface and these soon became exhausted and it was not until the late 15th and early 16th centuries that the deeper deposits could be reached. The Stannary towns of Chagford, Plympton and Tavistock became rich due to the revenue from the tin mines which have left interesting scars on the landscape. The mineral containing tin, which occurs on Dartmoor, is an oxide called cassiterite. Many regard Dartmoor's main characteristic as the tors but tin, the rarest of the base metals, has left an equally indelible mark. Some deposits were tapped in Cornwall as early as the Bronze Age but the earliest documentary evidence of tin mining in Devon comes from the Pipe Roll of 1156, when deposits of alluvial tin were extracted from Sheepstor and Brisworthy, both close to the source of the River Plym. Mining continued well into the 19th century and copper, lead, arsenic and iron were also extracted. The now deserted blowing houses are of particular interest as they give some idea of the smelting techniques.

In the early days of smelting the process was in two parts and it was the invention of the blowing house in the 13th century which enabled the task to be reduced to a single process. The old method involved heating the ore in a peat fire to produce impure tin which was full of grit and very lumpy. It was then taken by packhorse to smelting centres where it was further refined and cast into ingots, each Devon block weighing about 195 lbs (88.45 kg). It was then taken by packhorses throughout Britain and also exported by ships to the continent. During the late 12th century the richest tin deposits in the world were being mined on Dartmoor. A blowing house was virtually a set of bellows pumping air into the melting metal, and care had to be taken to stop the thatched roof catching fire. Occasionally the roof was fired on purpose to reclaim the particles which had been blasted into the air. Blowing houses usually had an attached or adjacent crushing and grinding mill, and were set into small hillsides and close to a stream. This was used to drive an overshot waterwheel which operated the bellows. The fuel for the fire was charcoal which accounts for the destruction of what was left of Dartmoor's woodland following the inroads made by Neolithic farmers. The molten metal was channelled out of the smelthouse into granite moulds.

Obviously tin was a vital mineral but what was it used for? Mixed with copper, bronze is produced and the fact that an age was named after the alloy is sure proof of its value. Bronze tools lasted longer and the cutting edge was considerably sharper than stone. Later in history bells were made of bronze and when mixed with lead, tin could be fashioned into the solder which was the stock-in-trade of travelling tinkers. Many domestic utensils were made of pewter which was an alloy of lead and tin whilst it is reliably documented that the monks used an amalgam of tin and saffron as a cheap alternative to using gold in their illuminated manuscripts. With the onset of electronic typesetting and new technology, printing presses no longer rely on the so-called hot metal processes with the characters made of a tin-based alloy. During this period the separate letters were kept in cases. Capitals were kept in an upper case and small letters in the lower case. We still retain these terms today even though metal typesetting is obsolete.

At one time jewelry and brooches were made from tin which was alloyed to resemble gold and there was also an important trade in Dartmoor tin to the courts of Europe where it was used to fashion coffins for the wealthy.

From pre-historic times, agriculture was also a vital occupation and Merrivale settlement, close to Princetown is a good example. The whole of this area of the moor is the habitat of the Dartmoor ponies who always delight the naturalist and sometimes frighten the motorist by strolling out in front of them. They seem to think they own the road and so they do – they were here first!

CHAPTER 2

Around Exeter

With a population of around 100,000 Exeter is the administrative centre of Devon but it can also lay claim to being the cultural centre. A short cut to discovering any city is to join a guided tour. Some are good and others not so good. Some are free and others are not. Exeter's tours are excellent, free and are available every day of the year except Christmas and Boxing Day. Each is led by a voluntary city guide. Details are available from the Tourist Information Centre and among the tours on offer include the Cathedral Close, Exeter Old and New, City to Riverside, the City Walls, Garden Tours and Exeter's Ghosts and Legends. In the summer there are a number of evening tours and it is possible with careful planning to enjoy three tours in one day with meal breaks in between. There are plenty of restaurants and inns including our favourite, the 14th century White Hart Hotel in South Street. Also medieval in origin are the Ship Inn and the Turk's Head where Dickens stayed and apparently watched the activities of the Fat Boy, who was used later in his writings.

A tour of any ancient city should begin at the Cathedral since it is invariably the oldest complete stone building to be found even though, as is the case with Exeter, some remnants of Roman occupation may exist. Exeter Cathedral, very much against the odds, survived the German bombs which rained down on the city during the Second World War, and the bulk of the Close which enfolds it, also escaped. Here the buildings are a history lesson in themselves and represent every architectural period from the medieval to the modern, and including a number of small churches. A fine Elizabethan House is now a jeweller's shop.

Beneath the Close is a Roman military bathhouse, which was one of the most sophisticated of the period, and which had exercise rooms plus hot and cold facilities. The complex was excavated between 1971 and 1973, but because of its position it could not be left exposed and was filled in with sand to protect it and then recovered.

Exeter Cathedral with its wonderful front.

An abbey was established in AD 670 by King Caennwealth and the present cathedral is on the same site. In the 9th century the Danes ransacked the area but eventually King Alfred expelled the invaders and set about providing the city with defensive walls. Exeter at this time had its own mint and the city became so dominant that in AD 1050 Bishop Leofric, appointed by Edward the Confessor, moved his see from Crediton which was described in our companion volume *Discovering Exmoor and North Devon*. The abbey which the Danes had destroyed was rebuilt and became the cathedral.

Peace did not last long, however, as the Normans set about consolidating their newly gained but still vulnerable kingdom. William the Conqueror was obliged to lay siege to Saxon-loyal Exeter and this 18 day confrontation is commemorated by a plaque on the wall of a wine shop on Longbrook Street. To underline their control the Normans built Rougemont Castle but on a more peaceful note they reconstructed the cathedral which was completed in 1206. The Lady chapel and the Chapter House date from this period but there was a major reconstruction during the 14th century.

There is a wealth of interesting furnishings in the Cathedral including the library now numbering more than 25,000 manuscripts and which was established by Leofric. The most treasured possession is the Exeter Book, an illuminated manuscript containing the largest collection of Anglo-Saxon poems in existence. Not to be outdone, the Normans are also well represented by an original and unique copy of the Domesday Book of 1086. This is a draft copy and contains details of lands and animal stocks which were not listed in the final volume. Then as now, authors must have found space at a premium.

In the Cathedral are a number of reminders of the early Bishops, obviously including Leofric but especially the tombs of Bronescombe, Stapeldon and Grandisson, a formidable trio who played a vital role in the construction and development of the cathedral during the 13th and 14th centuries. There is a huge 14th century Bishop's throne which looks to be made of stone, although it is actually made of wood. These days the throne looks plain, but in its hey-day it would have been brightly painted.

The choir stalls are also worth a long lingering look, especially the misericord carvings. One shows an elephant between a monk and a crusader and another a fierce looking crocodile swallowing its prey. The elephant is thought to be the first artistic representation of such a beast in England. There is a splendid 14th century minstrel's gallery in which an orchestra was situated in the days prior to the invention of the organ. In the north transept is a 15th century clock which shows the sun and moon in orbit round the earth. This was the accepted theory prior to the observations of Copernicus. It tells the hour and also the appropriate phase of the moon plus the inscribed motto "*pereunt et imputantur*" which means "the hours perish and are reckoned to our account". The Cathedral has a shop and a licenced refectory which is open from 10 am to 5 pm except on Sundays and guided tours are on offer also from Monday to Saturday.

The Cathedral is wonderfully impressive from the outside, especially the wide West Front with its twin Norman towers. The image screen is also a mightily impressive piece of carved stonework depicting angels, prophets, kings and soldiers. The statues read like a list of the Saxon and Norman peerage

Exeter Cathedral's astronomical clock photographed in the 1920s. It is very similar to the one at Ottery St Mary seen on page 127.

including Alfred, Athelstan, Canute and, of course, King William himself, all now protected from pigeon excreta by a complex of netting. The stone used is mainly Beer freestone, a granular limestone from the quarries near the chalk cliffs at Beer in East Devon. The characteristic of this pale stone is that it gets gradually paler with time. In the days before the Reformation, however, the screen would have been painted in bright colours much as we see in many Catholic countries of the modern-day Mediterranean.

Just like York and Norwich, Exeter not only has a splendid cathedral, but also a number of smaller churches whose origins take us back to the time before the growing city absorbed a number of smaller parishes, some dating to the days of the Saxon. There are seven in Exeter worth particular attention; St. Martin's, St. Petrock's, St. Mary Arches, the tiny St. Pancras, the ancient St. Olave's, St. Stephen's and St. Mary Steps. There is also the modern church of St. Michael's built in 1867 and whose spire is even more dominant from outside the town than the towers of the Cathedral.

St. Martin's is situated at the northern corner of the Cathedral Close, near to the Ship Inn which was apparently frequented by Sir Francis Drake on his visits to Exeter. The church is set at an angle to the street and this adds to its character and the interior is equally impressive and includes a 15th century barrel vaulted roof with carved bosses. Most of the building, however, dates to the 17th and 18th centuries and includes box-pews, a pulpit, some fine monuments and a magnificent gallery. Now as always St. Martin's is a busy looking church and its ecclesiastical finger is firmly on the pulse of commercial Exeter. St. Petrock's is on the eastern side of the close and although we do not find it so attractive as St. Martin's, it also has its own unique character and is one of a number in the West Country dedicated to Petrock, including the church next to Dartmouth Castle.

St. Olave's church on Fore Street is dedicated to Olaf the Christian Viking King who became the patron saint of Norway. Some historians believe that it originated as a house-chapel for King Canute's sister-in-law Gytha who was Countess of Wessex. The small square tower may well have been part of the original 11th century building.

St. Nicholas' Priory is reached from Fore Street along Mint Street, itself a reminder of Saxon times. Although the Benedictine House was dissolved on the orders of Henry VIII around 1536, a collection of its buildings remain. The house originated when William of Normandy gave the church of St. Olave's to Battle Abbey. It was the monks from the latter who built the Priory and the Norman undercroft remains almost unaltered and has been said to resemble a miniature

A wonderful Elizabethan house on Cathedral Close at Exeter. It is now a jeweller's shop.

version of the crypt at Canterbury cathedral. There is also a magnificent Guest Hall reached by a curved staircase and having a panelled screen. There is a Prior's room with his study situated in the tower and the so-called Tudor room with a decorated plaster ceiling. The kitchens have two huge 13th century fireplaces and the whole of the elegant building is constructed of red sandstone plus some contrasting brown stone called trap-rock. It has survived so well because it was a domestic residence for centuries, before being purchased by Exeter Corporation in 1913, since which time it has been intelligently restored. There is a small entry fee and the Priory is open Tuesday to Saturday from 10 am to 1 pm and 2 pm to 5.30 pm.

St. Mary Arches is said to be the most complete Norman church in Devon and is just off Fore Street. It takes its name from the double-chamfered Romanesque arches on either side of the nave and which pre-date any other similar structures to be found in Devon. Inside are some fascinating memorials including a 16th century tribute to Thomas Andrew, the master of the Guild of Merchant Adventurers and twice Mayor of Exeter. Thomas Walker was mayor three times and he and his wife are celebrated in memorial poem following his death in 1628.

St. Pancras is a tiny little church made to look even smaller by the towering bulk of department stores and a multi-storey car park all enclosing a pedestrianised precinct. The church is but a nave and a chancel built from rough but solid looking blocks of Heavitree stone dating to the 12th century but it is on the site of a much older Saxon structure. To the west is a small bell tower with the inscription on the bell itself summarising the effect of this pretty church. "Although I am small, I am heard over a great distance."

St. Stephen's is situated at the east end of the High Street and has beneath it an 11th century crypt. Following a disastrous fire in 1664 the church had to be rebuilt, and another massive reconstruction was essential following damage during the Second World War bombing.

St. Mary's Steps in West Street is constructed of sandstone and famous for its exterior 16th century clock and below this in a niche are the statues of Matthew the Miller and his two sons. The cobbled and steep roadway was the main medieval route from the west into the city and so it remained until 1778. Facing the church is a four storeyed timber framed building known as the 'House that Moved'. In 1961 it was blocking the route of a new road and rather than have it demolished it was jacked up and wheeled to a new position and thus saved for posterity. Near the West Gate is the old medieval sandstone

Exeter Sherriff's coach dating to around 1840 is in the foyer of the Civic Hall.

bridge which was damaged in the blitz, but carefully repaired in 1977.

The Guild Hall situated on High Street is one of the oldest such buildings in Britain. It was built in 1330, although it was substantially altered in the 15th century. There are arched and braced roof timbers resting on carved bosses showing bears holding staves. The first floor pillared front is Elizabethan with mullioned windows supported on an arcade extending over the pavement. Despite Victorian restoration the Hall is still splendid. In the gallery there is a cabinet full of civic silver and windows depicting prominent people with connections with Exeter including Princess Henrietta, the sister of Charles II, and the Civil War Parliamentarian, General Monk. Exeter has had a mayor since at least the 13th century and it is known that an earlier Guildhall existed, probably from around 1160. Thus Exeter's Lord Mayor has been established almost as long as London's and the two cities have had commercial and social links ever since. The Guildhall is open to the public except when it is required for civic business.

Close to the Guildhall is Parliament Street, said to be the narrowest street in the world. It was originally a medieval lane but its modern name dates to 1832 when the Reform Bill was passed. These days it connects the Guildhall Shopping Centre with the High Street.

Whilst the Guildhall was for the use of all tradesmen, the Tucker's Hall was the base for one particular trade. A Tucker was another name for a fuller, an occupation which involved the scouring and beating of woollen cloth during its final preparation. The workers had their own guild and what became their hall had its origins as a chapel dedicated by the Fraternity of Weavers, Fullers and Shearmen to the Blessed Virgin Mary. One of the prominent members in the 16th century was Sir Francis Drake's father, a rich merchant whose fortune was based upon woollen cloth. Exeter – indeed the whole of Devon – traded in woollens at least from the 13th century when a very rough material was woven, but as progress was made kersies, a light weight material, and then serges were produced until the 18th century. The local traders were then unable to compete with the huge textile mills in the North of England, which cornered the market and brought factory production to what had been a cottage industry. The religious fraternity only gave way to secular activities in the mid 16th century and Drake's father must have witnessed the transition. The present building, however, still retains some of its religious features. Additions to these included an upper floor. The barrel-vaulted roof was plastered between the beams and the walls were painted with frescoes, but in the 17th century some of these were covered up behind elaborate oak panelling. There are other carvings of a secular nature including some showing the guilds at work at teasel frames, bobbins, tuckers, shears and bales of cloth. Although the craftsmen have long gone their Guild Hall is maintained by donations made by businessmen members who enjoy dinners to which they invite the Liverymen from London.

If Exeter's textile history is impressive then so too is its Maritime Heritage and its museum is regarded as one of the most comprehensive in the world. In October 1991 the museum, despite its obvious excellence, ran into financial difficulties and only re-opened on April 1st 1992 after a

Exeter Maritime Museum is now open again and thriving.

winter of discontent and worry. It is well worth the entry fee and is open every day during the summer but closed in winter except by arrangement with the curator. The Maritime Museum advertises itself as a 'please touch museum' and this friendly atmosphere ensures a wonderful day out and should on no account be rushed. The best approach is from Crickle Pit Street and onto Quay Hill from which can be seen the old leats which once fed a complex of mills. During 1992 many of the old warehouses were converted into luxury dwellings. There are the massive Victorian warehouses, which have been adapted to hold the exhibits. When it opened in the 1960s the museum had only 23 craft, but since then the collection has grown and continues to grow and there are now more than 150 exhibits. Those range from dug-out canoes from Africa to one of the oldest steam vessels in the world. *Bertha*, designed by Brunel, was built in Bristol in 1844, continued to dredge mud from the Bridgewater Docks until 1964 and she is still in working order. The warehouses and some of the exhibits were used as sets for the classic television series *The Onedin Line* and the fact that many of the boats can be boarded adds to their attraction.

Visitors are transported across the River Exe to see a collection of Portuguese working boats plus the old Customs House built in 1681 and the old fish market which now houses a lifeboat.

The Exeter Quay House has also been opened as a museum, entry being free. There is an audio-visual display telling the history of Exeter over the last 2,000 years. It also concentrates on the River Exe and the construction of the Ship Canal. It opens daily except Christmas Day, Boxing Day and winter Fridays.

The Exeter Ship Canal was built in the 16th century because the Courtenay family of Powderham Castle, opposite Topsham, had constructed weirs across the river way back in 1285 and thus held river traffic to ransom. The presence of what became known as the Countessas Weir enabled Countess Isabella de Fortibus of Devon to force ships to discharge their cargo and then pay revenue to the family who owned the port of Topsham. The canal, probably the oldest in Britain, was built to combat this river closure and was cut from Topsham to the Custom House Quay in Exeter. It is certainly the oldest canal in Britain to feature locks and was opened in 1566 with further improvements being made in 1701 and 1830. John Trew was the engineer of the original waterway which was nearly two miles long and could cope with craft up to 16 tons. Eventually the facility was improved to such an extent that coasters of up to 400 tons can be accommodated. It now runs from Turf Lock on the Exe estuary, a distance of around 5 miles, to the Custom House passing through three locks. Topsham Lock provides a connection with the river which is crossed by a ferry. There are pretty and interesting walks along and around the canal towpath.

Topsham itself is well worth discovering and was an important harbour from the time of the Romans. It had a flourishing trade with Holland during the 15th, 16th and 17th centuries a period reflected in the Topsham Museum. This is housed in a late 17th century merchants house built in the Dutch style and has a substantial section devoted to Maritime History. In the old sail-loft is a natural history display concentrating on the birds of the Exe estuary including the rare avocet and greenshank plus the more common dunlin, knot, redshank, sanderling and ringed plover. The Topsham Society

Topsham is a fine example of an ancient harbour.

organise tours of the town and the Exe estuary each Wednesday and Saturday between May and September.

Although the Romans knew Topsham's sheltered harbour they also penetrated further up the Exe to what they knew as Isca Dumnoniorum which the Emperor Vespasian knew held a strategic position some 100 feet (30.4 metres) above the lowest fording point of the river. Here ships could tie up to a landing stage set in a break in the cliffs near where the Custom's House now stands. The Romans only took over a site which had been occupied for at least 200 years before their arrival by the Celtic tribe called the Dumnoaii and who called the fish-rich river Eisca. The line of Exeter's High Street lies on the line of the ancient track or Ridgeway. The Romans adapted the Celtic village and built their own town on the plateau and which conformed to their typical grid-iron pattern. Some small sections of the old Roman wall can still be seen and the best way to discover this is to join one of the Free Guided Walks mentioned at the beginning of this chapter. The walk takes about two hours and includes a visit to the sites of the former gates at the four points of the compass. Much of the original area of walls remain from Roman times to medieval times.

Just as fascinating as a tour of the city itself is a visit to the medieval network of underground passages, which were constructed around 1200 to bring freshwater into the city from a spring to the north. The work was instigated by the Dean and Chapter to supply the Cathedral but there was plenty for all who obtained their supply through a dipping hole. During the bombing of the Second World War the passages which stretch for more than 1/4 mile, proved to be a ready made shelter. A full renovation was carried out in 1989 and the passages, reached from the east end of Southernhay, were re-opened to the public on payment of a small fee. The passages are very narrow and anyone suffering from claustrophobia may want to give them a miss.

Exeter has two particularly fine museums. Rougemont House only opened in 1987, but has already taken its place on the city's Heritage Trail. It has an excellent collection of costume and lace. Adjoining the house are the Northenhay Gardens in which grow palms and other exotic plants. Also nearby is the outer bailey of the once extensive Roughemont Castle built by the Normans of red sandstone. The only substantial remnant is the gatehouse. It is open from Monday to Saturday from 10 am to 5.30 pm although it stays open longer in summer. There is a small entry fee but on Fridays this is waived.

The Royal Albert Memorial Museum is the official city museum and has exhibitions of local archeology and history as well as collections of silver and paintings. There are also ethnogeographical displays including Eskimos and North American Indians and in the summer there are exhibitions and holiday activities for children. The museum opens from Tuesday to Saturday from 10 am to 5.30 pm and entry is free.

The department of Leisure and Tourism have done a great deal of recent work in setting up a number of valley parks at Mincinglake, Ludwell, Duryard and the largest which is the Riverside Valley Park and which runs from the Canal Basin to Topsham Ferry. These provide an easy route from the heart of the city to the glories of the countryside. From the valley there are a number of circular walks leading through delightful scenery rich in wildlife and we have found plenty of interest in each of the four seasons. In spring we have listened to singing blackcap, nuthatch, wood warbler and chiff-chaff whilst making

The common lizard is often seen sunning itself on the rocks of Devon.

a list of spring flowers including primrose, dog violet, wood sorrel and coltsfoot. In the summer we listed weasel, stoat, fox, slow worm and a splendid common lizard sunning itself on a fallen branch of a tree. There is a great variety of butterflies including small tortoiseshell, comma, common blue, meadow brown, grayling and brimstone. In autumn red admirals are often to be found and there are some rich crops of blackberry and crab apple. During winter we often search for old nests of birds which are used by small mammals such as the wood mouse which are active throughout the winter and build up food stores of berries and nuts to see them through the colder months. The small mammals are in turn hunted by tawny owls which roost in the trees which grow well in the river valleys.

In the Duryard valley there is a picnic site off Pennsylvania Road from which there are views across to Dartmoor. Within range of the city by car there are a number of interesting places including Powderham and Chudleigh.

Powderham Castle lies snug and close to the west bank of the Exe and to the south of Exeter. It dates from the 1390s when the de Courtenay family moved from France with Eleanor of Aquitaine the Queen of Henry II. They were given the manor at this time and have been there ever since. In the 15th century Sir Philip Courtenay was the Lord Lieutenant of Ireland and later the family rose to become the Earls of Devon. The house was enlarged and altered in the 18th century and inside are many good paintings including family portraits by Reynolds. In the park are some wonderful old oaks which provide shelter for a herd of deer. Powderham is open in the afternoons from Sunday to Thursday between May and September.

Chudleigh is a delightful market town close to which is Ugbrook House, a rather ugly name for a truly beautiful building. In the town are some attractive Georgian houses, but the main attraction is the Wheel Community Craft Centre based at the Old Town Mills which were driven by a huge waterwheel now accurately restored. Around this there are the workshops of blacksmiths, potters, toy-makers, leather and textile artisans and other craftsmen. There is a craft shop in which the goods produced are sold.

Just to the south west of the town are the Chudleigh Rocks, which are weirdly shaped outcroppings of limestone. One is called the Pope's Head and legend has it that if a pin stuck in it does not fall out then a wish will be granted. There is also a so-called Pixie Hole.

Ugbrook House is open every afternoon from Spring Bank Holiday to September and holds a varied and fascinating collection of portraits, uniforms, silver, furniture and of special interest is a display of embroidery. It was built in the late 18th century for the 4th Lord Clifford of Chudleigh and, as at Powderham, the original family are still in residence. This gives both houses a real feeling of being lived in. Robert Adam was employed to produce a castle-like appearance and this was his first successful venture into this area of architecture.

One needs to drive to discover these joys but on the eastern outskirts of Exeter is Bowhill, a fine manor house with a magnificent timbered roof. Beyond this is a hill from which there are splendid views of Exeter and the A30. The latter is one of the best access routes to Dartmoor and forms part of the next chapter.

CHAPTER 3
Around Dartmoor

In this chapter we shall use Exeter as a base for a circular drive around Dartmoor. The route follows the A38 from Exeter through Ashburton, Buckfastleigh, South Brent, Ivybridge and then swings away from Plymouth to Tavistock, along the A386 and continues to Okehampton. From Okehampton the A30 returns to Exeter. We have also varied this route whilst staying at Plymouth and there are many points from which diversions can be made into the heart of Dartmoor. This central area will be described in chapter four.

Now bypassed by the A38 Ashburton has almost returned to the comparative peace of its past before motor vehicles jammed its narrow streets. But not quite, as its attractions as a shopping and tourist centre are all too apparent. It is set on the southern edge of Dartmoor and surrounded by hills through which flows the pretty River Ashburn on its tumbling way to join the Dart below Dart Bridge. The spirit of Dartmoor hovers around in the form of the bare, gaunt yet attractive tors of granite. A visit at the time of the June festival will reveal that much of the ancient human spirit is alive and well. At this time the town buzzes with folklore, fable, fact and fun.

The area was settled before the Saxons came but from then there is a continuous line. There was a market which was supervised by an officer called a Portreeve who was appointed by the monarch. He was charged to ensure the regulation of the sale of cattle and property and to preside over the Court Leet which was a judicial assembly. The Portreeve was indeed a powerful official. The tradition is maintained at Ashburton to the present day although it is purely ceremonial these days. On the fourth Tuesday in November officials meet at the chapel of St. Lawrence and the Court Crier announces a group of officers who are duly sworn in. These are Bread Weighers, Ale Tasters, Pig Drovers and very much in tune with modern day green issues they even have a Viewer of Watercourses. Some of these duties may seem to us to be of minor importance but the

Bread Weighers and Ale Tasters were the Weights and Measures Officers of their day and they ensured that folk got value for money. The Pig Drovers ensured that all citizens could freely graze their pigs on the acorns found in the local woodlands. The Viewer of Watercourses was probably more concerned with the availability of water than its purity but there were important industries in and around Ashburton which used – and misused – water.

Tin and wool were both vital industries and as early as 1285 Ashburton was one of four stannary towns in Devon, the others being Chagford, Tavistock and Plympton. To these towns the tin was brought down from the moors and was weighed, stamped and the necessary duty was paid. The tinners, like the goldminers of the Klondyke, then stocked up with food and other essential provisions before returning to their moorland workings. Thus the stannary towns attracted merchants and other essential service industries. At the same time the woollen trade was thriving and Ashburton cloth was exported as far as China and transported by the East India Company. The mill wheels were powered by the swift running River Ashburn and the town became very wealthy with some of the substantial profits diverted to build an impressive church. Other comparatively less important industries were the quarrying of marble which continued until 1970, and the mining of umber and ochre which were used as paint pigments. There were also small but workable deposits of iron and arsenic. For a while there was also a high quality pewter industry in the town. Pewter is a grey alloy of tin and lead which was used in the production of eating utensils and also for a while in the manufacture of bells hung around the neck of the leading horse during the days of the packhorse traffic.

The parish church of St. Andrew's was almost entirely reconstructed during the 15th century as each of the prosperous wool merchants looked over their shoulders at money given by their competitors and were determined not to be outdone. The tall slender tower is magnificent and framed by evergreen trees which makes it difficult to photograph from some angles. The interior is a good example of the work of G. E. Street but he had the good sense to leave alone a couple of wooden roofs – one flat and the other of a wagon type. In the town there are

Ashburton church clearly showing the turret staircase and taken about 1920.

a couple of particularly interesting buildings. Number 4 North Street was once the 'Mermaid Inn' already well established by the time of the Civil Wars of the 1640s when it was used by General Fairfax as his headquarters. The small, but very compact and informative, town museum is situated in what has become known as the Little House on West Street.

Ashburton can be used as a focus for the exploration of delightful villages including Buckland-on-the-Moor and Holne which are separated by a road cutting through a lovely area of woodland overlooking the River Webburn. Another rich area of woodland abounding with wildlife is situated about 1/4 mile from Holne and set upon a slope overlooking the River Dart. Holne Woods are looked after by the National Trust and here we watched a treecreeper building its nest behind a section of loose bark on an old birch tree, below which grew succulent and delicately yellow primroses and white wood sorrel. Holne Park is now the base for the River Dart Country Park which has a cafe, self service shop, self catering units, a camping and caravan site plus an adventure playground. It is open daily from April to September and apart from "action areas" for the young there are secluded areas and nature trails. Holne village itself is attractive and the author the Revd. Charles Kingsley (1819–1875), who wrote the *Water Babies* (1863) and *Westward Ho!* (1855), was born in the vicarage. The church here and at Buckland-on-the-Moor are both 13th century with alterations carried out in the 15th century. They are both noted for the painted panels on their medieval screens and the two should really be visited on the same day. We suggest Holne in the morning followed by a picnic lunch in Holne Woods and then on to Buckland-on-the-Moor in the afternoon. Holne derives its name from the holly tree which is one of the slowest growing of British trees, and was very popular as logs for burning and also as a decoration at Christmas. It was once the Holy Tree used at Christmas much as we use spruce these days.

There is also a 15th century bridge built high over the river and has indentations in which pedestrians once stood to be safe from packhorse traffic. The old bridge is still in use and the V-shaped indentations are ideal places for bird watchers to avoid cars and to observe the river, the breeding ground for common sandpiper, dipper and grey wagtail. Nearby is Holne Chase Camp, a circular earthwork which is a single rampart and ditch dating to the Iron Age. The surrounding area is a rich hunting area for naturalists and here are birches beneath which grow the fungus fly agaric one of the most beautiful species to be found in Britain. It is red with white blotches and has a typical mushroom shape. In medieval times the fungus was boiled in milk and placed in the room of a sick person. Flies attracted to the brew were poisoned and 'agaric' actually means poisonous. Alder grows well in the area and in winter its seeds are fed upon by long tailed tits. Nearby New Bridge, despite its name, is also medieval and is even narrower than Holne. The area around New Bridge marks the division between lowland and moorland conditions and the home of buzzard, green woodpecker, nuthatch, marsh tit and even the occasional kingfisher. The damp climate produces the perfect habitat for frogs and dragonflies.

Buckfastleigh is another small market town full of character and interest and set on the old highway between Exeter and Plymouth. Originally Buckfast Abbey, a mile or so up river, was the focus of local settlement and it was this which stimulated

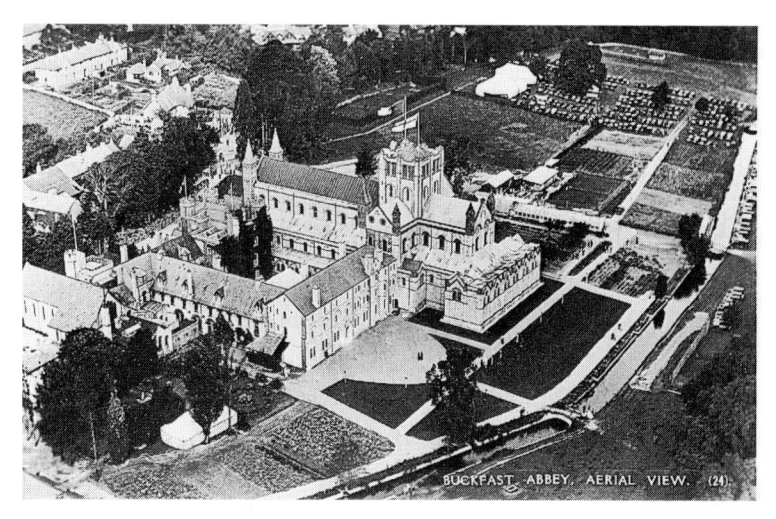

Buckfast Abbey, photographed from the air, about 1935, is one of the wonders of the 20th century.

the development of Buckfastleigh which means "the clearing at Buckfast". Here the parish church dates to the 13th century although there were substantial alterations and additions made in the 15th century. Few Devon churches are more attractively sited having been built on top of a limestone outcrop and reached via a steep narrow cobbled route of 196 steps. The climb is well worth the effort for the view from the churchyard is truly dramatic. In the churchyard itself are the ruins of an old chantry chapel which is said to have had a Pardoner's room above it. A Pardoner was one with permission from the Pope to sell pardons or indulgencies, a practice which ceased after the Reformation. In the churchyard there is also a mausoleum covering the grave of Richard Cabell who died in 1677 and whose evil life may have influenced Sir Arthur Conan Doyle when he was working on his book *The Hound of the Baskervilles*. Richard Cabell lived at Brook Manor situated about a mile to the north west and close to the moor on the banks of the Mardle river. He had a reputation for seducing young girls which was probably deserved and also of being in league with the devil which probably he was not. Local legend describes huge fire-breathing black dogs around his tomb and children were told not to poke their fingers into the chinks in the tomb or Richard was more than likely to drag them in. This was the stuff of novels and Conan Doyle was never one to miss a golden opportunity of including black fire-breathing dogs, boggy moorlands and thick grey hanging mists.

No church looks as solid as Holy Trinity, but appearances can be deceptive because the limestone rock on which it stands is riddled with a network of caves. This, like the area around Torquay, is caving country. The Buckfastleigh system was first investigated by the Revd. J. MacEnery in the 1820s and then by William Pengelly both of whom had studied other systems including Kents Cavern described in chapter 7. The William Pengelly Cave Studies Centre has been established in Higher Kiln Quarry and this was set up to conduct scientific research. It is also the haunt of bats, especially Natterers and the Lesser Horseshoe. The Centre is open to the public but the times are not regular since it is staffed by volunteers. The caves, being bat roosts, are now protected by law and they are not considered safe unless the visitor is accompanied by an experienced caver. Although bats are the present occupants there is evidence of previous species which lived in the area thousands of years ago, during the warm interglacial periods which separated the Ice Ages. Species identified include bison, hippopotamus, hyena, lion and giant red and fallow deer. All this again proves that Devon once had a climate which resembled the conditions found in Africa at the present time.

Buckfastleigh is the headquarters and terminus of the South Devon Railway which runs a 14 mile round trip along the valley of the River Dart towards Totnes. Like many other branch lines it was closed during the Beeching Cuts of the early 1960s but was reopened by steam enthusiasts in 1969. There is now a regular service between June and September with some trains running in late March, April, May and October and there is a steam museum. At Christmas Santa by Steam is a real treat for the children. The Dart rises high on Dartmoor and becomes tidal just outside Totnes close to the station at Littlehempston Riverside. From near here there are fine views of the river and of Totnes castle. Much of the river valley visible from the train cannot be seen any other way and is the haunt of badger,

A postcard of the 1920s showing the brothers of Buckfast Abbey at work.

fox, heron and breeding mute swans. The other station on the line is at Staverton which was once important to local folk as it transported their cider brewed on the farms to market. The Primrose Line is a registered charity and almost all its friendly staff are volunteers.

For an extra fee passengers can travel in the luxury provided by a first class coach once part of the Great Western Railway's Paddington to Plymouth *Ocean Express*. This is a reminder of the great days of steam powered liners and locomotives.

For those who find a study of bones and bats a little dry and brown then a visit to the Buckfast Butterfly Farm and Dartmoor Otter Sanctuary will restore a sense of excitement and colour. The butterflies may be seen and photographed between mid March and November and the otters are at home to visitors from early March to mid-November. There is an entry fee but parking is free and there is a large picnic area and a gift shop. There is an accurately designed tropical rain forest with ponds, waterfalls and bridges providing the perfect habitat for the exotic butterflies and the visitors who come to visit and photograph them. This area and the South Devon Railway are so close together that the two can be combined to produce a wonderful day of discovery.

The Primrose Line at Buckfastleigh getting steam up for a day's work.

Buckfast Abbey was founded by King Canute in 1018 as a Benedictine House, its brothers dressing in black habits but it later converted to the more austere rule of the white-robed Cistercians. They remained until the house was dissolved on the orders of Henry VIII in 1539. In 1796 the old abbey was a sad ruin, and in 1806 a private house was built using much of the masonry. Had not a community of French Benedictine monks, displaced from their native house, bought Buckfast in 1886 its history would have crumbled away. The new Benedictines, however, worked a modern miracle. Six monks, only one of whom had any building experience, set about building an abbey in 1907 and their church was completed by 1937. Abbot Vonier was in charge of the project and Brother Peter, the Mason, did the actual construction. The abbot died soon after the church was completed but Brother Peter lived on until the 1960s, by which time many more fine buildings had been added and Buckfast was placed firmly on the tourist map. The abbey now dominates the village just as it did during the Middle Ages. The main feature of the church is the magnificent east window in the chapel of the Blessed Sacrament, a tribute to the glass worker Father Charles. The abbey is open daily throughout the year from 5.30 in the morning to 9 in the evening and all services are open to the public. There is a sung mass each Sunday and on Holy Days of Obligation at 10.30 am and on other days at 8 am. Other masses are said on Sundays and Holy Days of Obligation at 9 am and 7.15 pm and on other days at noon. There is a car and coach park with shops selling Buckfast Tonic Wine, honey produced by the world famous bee keeper Brother Adam and books plus other gifts. There is a licenced refreshment room, an audio visual presentation telling the history of the abbey from AD 1016 to the present day and a unique collection of photographs showing the building of the modern abbey. No doubt it was the monks who established a healthy trade in wool and this was the staple industry of Buckfastleigh until well into the present century. The mills are sited on the banks of the small but swift moving River Mardle which turned their wheels. In the 16th century Buckfastleigh was, in the context of the period, a place of heavy industry with seven woollen mills plus a paper mill, a tannery, limestone quarries and lime burning as well as some tin mining in the surrounding area. No doubt the Cistercians had a great financial interest in all these enterprises, and in farming especially sheep rearing.

Buckfastleigh has plenty of archeological and historical interest but it also has an important literary association. One mile beyond the town and close to the A38 is Dean Prior, the one time home of Robert Herrick (1591–1674) a London born cleric who worked in Devon despite the fact that he had no love for the county, an opinion he expressed in rhyme:-

"More discontents I never had
Since I was born than here;
Where I have been and still am sad
In this dull Devonshire."

An ardent Royalist, Herrick was displaced from his post on the orders of Parliament in 1647 but he was reinstated following the Restoration of Charles II in 1660 and remained in office until his death. A brief consideration of Herrick's life history will perhaps allow us to understand his unease with the rural life of Devonshire, although he must have had some days when the exuberance of the local peasantry must have stirred his soul.

Robert was the seventh child of a well-to-do Leicester goldsmith who moved his shop to London, the birthplace of his wife Julia, the daughter of a Mercer. In 1592 when Robert was only 16 months old his father fell to his death from a window only a couple of days after making his will. Although suicide was suspected there was sufficient doubt to prevent the Queen's Almoner from confiscating his estate which was the practice in those days. This prevented the family from becoming paupers and it would seem that young Robert was given a sound early education. It is certain that in 1607 he was apprenticed to his uncle Sir William Herrick of Leicester, who was also a goldsmith. In 1613 the ambitious young man obtained a release from his apprenticeship and was admitted to St. John's College Cambridge as a Fellow Commoner, which meant that he paid double fees and ate at high table. This proves that his uncle was not only wealthy but generous. Later Robert moved to Trinity Hall probably to cut down expenses. He obtained his B.A. in 1617, M.A. in 1620 and in 1623 he was ordained. At this time Robert Herrick the poet was beginning to make his name in literary circles.

Taking up a post at Dean Prior must have made him feel isolated from the world of scholarship and this was expressed in his writings. He eventually deserted his post much to the disappointment and annoyance of his Bishop and he lived for a time in Westminster with a girl named Tomasin Parsons. She was 27 years younger than Herrick and probably bore him a daughter. Apart from the disruption following the Civil War his last years were spent back in Devon and as he got older a degree of eccentricity seems to have developed. He kept a pet pig which he took for walks and taught it to drink beer from a tankard. Herrick died at Dean Prior but the grave of one of England's most important early poets is unmarked. His work certainly deserves more recognition than it has so far received.

The next large settlement on the A38 is South Brent which belonged to the Cistercian monks of Buckfast until the Dissolution and in 1546 it was purchased by Sir William Petre of Torbryan. The church, fringed by venerable old trees is sited close to the River Avon and almost astride an ancient trackway. Part of its Saxon tower remains and there are examples of each subsequent style of architecture. Inside is a red sandstone font dating to the 11th century and on the outside of the door is a sanctuary knocker, one of several to be found in Devonshire. The parish controlled a large area of what is now South Hams as well as a substantial part of Dartmoor described in chapters five and four respectively. Here there was a regular market as well as an occasional but very important fair and an annual horse sale when Dartmoor ponies were rounded up in what became known as 'the drift'. Dartmoors are still the most popular of childrens' ponies.

In 1556 South Brent was given the status of a Borough and it later became an important centre for the production of woollens and some of the solid looking mills still stand on the river. As a couple who have spent much of their working life among the textile mills of Lancashire and Yorkshire, these Devon factories are smaller and more attractive than we expected.

Set, as we have seen, on an ancient track, South Brent initially became rather isolated when the railways pushed their way through the Devon countryside. Although the Great Western Railway passed through Brent in 1848 there was no link to Kingsbridge until 1893. After this the Devon link was complete and South Brent became a vital junction between the main lines bound for Plymouth, Cornwall and Exeter.

Like South Brent, Ivybridge was also reached by railway as Brunel pushed the South Devon railway across the Erme valley in 1848 by means of a magnificent viaduct, although only a few of the original pillars remain following a solid stone reconstruction in 1895. We cannot regret this as much of Brunel's early structure was of timber. The best way to view Ivybridge is to climb Westgate Hill where there was a Bronze Age settlement, reached by a footpath leading upwards from close to the bridge over the A38. Although Ivybridge is a modern and still developing town, its bridge is ancient and listed as Ponte Ederaso in 1250, although by 1292 the name had changed to Ivybrigge. This was an essential crossing of the River Erne and was at the centre of four ancient parishes of Cornwood, Harford, Ugborough and Ermington, a most fascinating quartet.

Cornwood lies on the Yealm, which has been dammed in the grounds of Blachford Park and is snuggled into the fold of a hill protecting it from the stiff winds which blast down off the moors. Fardel Manor has also been similarly landscaped and is situated between Cornwood and Ivybridge. Here is another settlement which evolved alongside an ancient trackway, this time between the Rivers Erme and Plym. A standing stone with an ancient inscription was situated nearby, but alas this was not left in situ, but removed to the clinical and souless atmosphere of the British Museum. Although the house is not open to the public it has been restored and looks truly magnificent, especially the 16th century porch, guarded by rampant stone lions and leopards.

Harford consists of a farm, a huddle of neat cottages and a small 16th century granite church which is famous for a set of brasses commemorating the life of Thomas Williams (1513–1566) who came from nearby Stowford and who became the Speaker of the House of Commons. There is a pretty track which follows the River Erme down to Ivybridge an area full of delightful trees, especially around Stowford Cleave. Here the river tumbles in a torrent of white water over a mass of rocks. High above the east bank is Stowford Lodge, part of a manor mentioned in Domesday and now used as a Conference Centre for the Royal Agricultural Society of England. Below this is Stowford Paper Mill which was first established in 1787 by a miller from Plymouth named William Dunsterville. The waters of the Erme are soft and still so free of pollutants that it was ideal for the manufacture of paper, an industry which continues to the present day.

Ugborough church is noted for its carved roof bosses including rabbits and also a sow with her litter which is known to have been an ancient fertility symbol. Those who love wood carvings should also visit Ermington's church which is a delight, a uniqueness compounded by its slightly leaning spire. There was a Celtic and then a Saxon settlement here and it is also mentioned in Domesday. The present church dates mainly from the 14th century and nobody interested in wood carving can afford to miss it. Naturalists will not be disappointed either as the scenes depicted show life in the forest and include owls both perched and in flight, squirrels, deer, rabbits, mice and voles and some really slimy looking snakes. Foreign species are also represented including monkeys. The carvings are not medieval and more than ample proof that the Victorians had their own master craftsmen or in this case craftswomen. Violet Pinwell, the daughter of the rector, and her six daughters set about carving in the church around 1880. This is no mere parochial work as Violet was a well known teacher of the craft and who had studios in Plymouth which employed many craftspeople. Their work was much in demand throughout the west country. The Ermington collection, however, deserves much more praise than it has ever been given.

After Ivybridge the next major settlement is Tavistock, one of our favourite bases from which to discover the glories of Devon. Since Saxon times it has dominated the west side of Dartmoor. Around the town are the beautiful river valleys of the Tamar, Tavy and Lyd. From the first Saxon camp or Stock on the Tavy, Tavistock has grown into the largest town in West Devon and we should not allow it to be overshadowed by the city of Plymouth which is only about 10 miles away. Tavistock has three markets; each Tuesday there is an antique and craft market which is popular with both locals and visitors the latter in search of typical ornaments of the area to remind them of their holiday. On Wednesdays the Victorian market is also well worth a visit, especially for photographers, as many stallholders wear the dress of the period. But the real historical gem is the Pannier market held each Friday since its establishment in 1105. This was when Abbot Osbert of the abbey was given

A postcard of Morwellham Quay taken about 1870.

permission by Henry I to hold a market outside its gates. Like the Pannier market at Barnstaple, which we described in our companion volume *Discovering Exmoor and North Devon*, it derived its name from the fact that local folk travelled in to market carrying their goods in baskets or panniers.

Tavistock as a town, actually grew up around the Benedictine Abbey which was founded in AD 974 and by the time of its dissolution it was the wealthiest monastery in Devon. The original site was skillfully chosen and the Benedictines knew well how to attract benefactors and the pity is that so little of the once magnificently rich establishment remains. The foundations of the long demolished church now lie below Bedford Square and the Chapter House and cloisters below Plymouth Road. Although Henry VIII's Commissioners allowed the dismantling of the fabric of the abbey, most of its grounds passed into the hands of John Russel, then a squire who was President of the Council of the West and who later became the Earl of Bedford. His ancestors, elevated to the rank of Duke, did much to bring prosperity to Tavistock. There are, however, a few impressive remains of the old abbey including what has become known as

The staff of Morwellham Quay always work in period costume.

'Betsy Grimbal's Tower' the name of which many guide books suggest has no known origin. The excellent little Town Trail Guide, however, is much more helpful and points out that it is the Old Great Western Gate of both the abbey and Tavistock town. It includes part of the Abbot's lodging built in the 15th century and the name is a corruption of 'The Blessed Grimwald' who was a 9th century saint. Also still standing is the abbey chapel, a rather misleading name for a building which was actually the monks' refectory. The abbey bridge is not contemporary with the monastery being constructed of Dartmoor granite in 1860, but probably replacing a more ancient span. Another building which relates to the abbey is the Ordulph Arms which commemorates the abbot of that

The old water wheel at Morwellham Quay.

name who rebuilt the monastery following its destruction by the Danes in the 11th century. The Court Gate was the main entrance to the abbey and was restored in 1824 some years before the construction of the adjacent Bedford Square. Here is a fine example of Victorian town architecture. The Guildhall and Town Hall are overlooked by a fine statue in greenish volcanic stone of Frances, the 7th Duke of Bedford, who was responsible for the remodeling of the town centre. This was the Duke's way of giving something back to an area which had provided him with a vast fortune from local deposits of copper ore which reached a peak during the mid 19th century.

A reminder of this golden age is to be found at nearby Morwellham Quay which was at that time Britain's largest copper exporting harbour. The Quay can be reached by following the A390 Tavistock to Liskeard road and bearing left along the well signed road after a distance of around two miles. The Quay and its fittings would have crumbled away long ago following the decline of copper mining had it not been restored by the Morwellham Trust, which diverts entry fees and other funds directly to the upkeep and conservation of the Quay. Visitors can watch and even converse with working coopers, blacksmiths and quay workers who are often dressed in the costume of the period. Here, on a cold breezy day in late March, we met Gary Emerson, elegantly dressed in his Victorian garb and over a warming cup of hot chocolate discussed the history and the ambitions of the Trust. It is even possible for the visitors themselves to try on clothes from a wardrobe of the 1860s. They can then travel by horse and carriage along the Duke of Bedford's country trackway, a route followed by Queen Victoria in 1856. Another exciting journey of about half-a-mile on an electric tramway leads first along the banks of the River Tamar and then deep into the bowels of the George and Charlotte Copper mine. Here is an accurate reconstruction of the conditions endured by the miners in 1868. The sound of the giant waterwheel which kept the mine dry throbs away and adds authentic sound. Morwellham Quay is open every day of the year except the period 23rd December to 1st January. In summer it opens from 10 am to 5.30 pm with the last entry at 3.30 pm. In winter it closes at 4.30 pm with the last entry at 2.30 pm. The Ship Inn restaurant and tea rooms has a table licence and is open from Easter to December. To us the 150 acres (60 hectares) which make up this Victorian industrial village is one of the finest attractions to be found in Devon. Apart from the obvious reminders of mining there are also splendid woodland walks and the Morwell Rocks are another attraction.

Tavistock and Morwellham were once connected by a canal, the towpath of which can be followed until the cut disappears into a tunnel. It was constructed between 1803 and 1817 and

Old ships and the quay at Morwellham in the process of restoration.

until it closed in 1887 provided Tavistock with a link into the Tamar and thence to the sea. It carried mineral ore from the Mary Tavy mines in one direction with coal and fertiliser passing along in the reverse direction. At Morwellham the canal ends some 240 feet (73.1 metres) above the quay and the barges were raised and dropped via an inclined plane operated by a windlass powered by water.

Tavistock can also be used as a centre from which to explore the surrounding area including Cotehele Quay, Gunnislake and Yelverton. Cotehele Quay should be explored during the same period as Morwellham as the two complement each other and reflect the rôle of the River Tamar as a commercial water. The restored quayside at Cotehele is impressive and set into a gentle loop of the river and was frequented by those employed in the mining and quarrying industries. The National Trust have worked wonders here and the museum reflects the days when lime and coal was unloaded whilst going out were tin, lead and especially copper plus barrels of arsenic. Who knows what damage was done to the health of the workers prior to the laws being passed to protect them. Not far from the two quays is Gunnislake where a medieval bridge spans the Tamar and here is a boundary between Devon and Cornwall.

Yelverton is another pretty and interesting place which is worth a visit just to see the Paperweight Centre opposite the Leg O' Mutton which serves excellent bar snacks. There are hundreds of paperweights on display of all shapes, sizes and colours with some being modern but others valuable antiques. Here is yet another chance to buy that special memento. The centre also sells oil paintings and watercolours. It is open from March to November, Monday to Saturday from 10 am to 5 pm and all winter on Wednesday from 1 pm to 5 pm and Saturday 10 am to 5 pm. It will open at other times by appointment. Yelverton is right on the edge of Dartmoor and the gorse covered surrounding hills especially Roborough Common are breeding grounds for such birds as stonechat, whinchat, linnet and long-tailed tit and in wintry weather the scrub provides shelter for sheep and Dartmoor ponies. Both Yelverton itself and nearby Crapstone have become popular as retirement or holiday villages as they are both within easy travelling distance of Plymouth. In one sense this influx has priced young people out of the market and some of the living-working atmosphere they once possessed has been lost. Flowing in the opposite direction is water which is pumped from Burrator reservoir below Sheepstor to slake the thirst of Plymouth. Some historians believe that it was Sir Francis Drake who was the first to construct a leet to provide drinking water for Plymouth and the mayor of Burrator still proposes a toast at the annual *Fishing Feaste* and hopes that 'the descendants of him who brought us water never want wine.'

Drake himself lived at Buckland Abbey two miles to the west and enclosed in a sheltered dell close to the River Tavy. It was not uncommon after the Reformation for monasteries to be converted into private houses, but Drake's home was constructed from the church itself and this is most unusual. The abbey was founded by the Cistercians in 1278 and following the Dissolution in the late 1530s it first passed into the hands of the seaman Sir Richard Grenville, whose mammoth exploits

Around Burrator reservoir and Sheepstor is some of the finest scenery in Devon.

in his little ship *Revenge* were almost as dramatic as those of Drake himself. In 1581 Sir Francis bought the abbey from his rival which must have given him great pleasure and the abbey church tower still dominates the house. The dining room was panelled according to Drake's instructions and Buckland Abbey remained in the hands of the Drake family until 1947 when its stewardship was taken over by the National Trust. They now lease the house to Plymouth Corporation. It is open throughout the year. The most famous exhibit is Drake's Drum which was retrieved by his brother Thomas who was with Sir Francis when he died of dysentry in 1596 on the Spanish Main. The Drum was made the subject of a patriotic poem published in 1895 and written by Sir Henry John Newbolt (1862–1938). The medieval tithe barn at Buckland is one of the finest in the country and is large enough to hold a comprehensive collection of carts and carriages. It is however, the maritime exhibits, especially those with Drake connections which attracts, but the house itself, still looking stately and monastic, is a photographer's delight.

There are areas in the surrounding countryside which Drake himself would probably still recognise and which show off South West Devon at its most beautiful. Rasborough Down and the Walkham Valley with its steeply sloping woodlands and riverside paths are sharply contrasting and exciting places in which to enjoy a leisurely picnic. Whilst writing our companion volume *Discovering Coastal Yorkshire* we described Cook's country and we could see great similarities with Drake's country, the two having bracingly breezy uplands and sheltered and unpolluted river valleys. Such countryside must have kept the morale of the mariners high at times when they were becalmed in the tropics or battered by life-threatening storms. Lydford, reached along the A386 via Mary Tavy is another place offering wonderful walks especially the $1\frac{1}{2}$ mile long Lydford Gorge owned by the National Trust and famous for the White Lady Waterfall and the heaving Devil's Cauldron separated by some calmer stretches of water which offer great sport to anglers and birdwatchers. Common sandpiper breed here although the species is not so common on and around Dartmoor as in other parts of Britain. There is plenty of parking in the area and some excellent and well signed forest walks.

Although now quiet and lying at the western edge of Dartmoor, Lydford was once a vital link in the Kingdom of Wessex, governed by Alfred the Great. Although the settlement was never walled it was protected by an earthen rampart. The Normans took over the town and built a fort just to the west of the church but this was soon abandoned when the castle was built in 1195. Its great keep was intended to imprison those

The White Lady Waterfall at Lydford.

The Museum of Water Power at Sticklepath.

Saxons foolish enough to transgress the forest and stannary laws.

The parish church dedicated to St. Petrock, is probably on the site of a wooden Saxon structure dating to the 7th century. The font is possibly Saxon and the little town itself is based on a Saxon grid. The Castle Inn was once called the White Horse and it is said that the beast so remembered managed to leap across Lydford gorge whilst carrying its owner from Plymouth to Okehampton.

There are good hotels in Yelverton including the Moorland Links and the Saddler's Retreat Country House on Tavistock road, but for our discovery tour around Dartmoor we always prefer to use Tavistock.

Once the various bits of Tavistock Abbey have been located, some time can be spent exploring the huge parish church of St. Eustachius. It was probably the presence of such a dominant church which caused the demise of the abbey. In towns where the people were allowed to worship with the monks and had no church of their own Henry's commissioners allowed the abbey church to survive. At Tavistock, however, there already was a fine parish church and so down came the splendid abbey. Perhaps the magnificence of the latter accounts for what many writers have described as the plain and austere nature of the mainly 15th century St. Eustachius. The lack of rich ornamentation, however, may also be due to the fact that the real prosperity of Tavistock did not come until the 19th century copper boom which made a fortune for the Duke of Bedford. Some earlier prosperity, however, did accrue from wool and from tin mining. We feel that St. Euchachius has had a bit of a raw deal from ecclesiastical writers and there are few carvings found in the west country so attractive as the pink alabaster monument to the lawyer Sir John Glanville which dates to 1600 and the soaring narrow aisles of the church itself are without doubt attractive. The windows in the north aisle are an excellent example of the work of William Morris.

No visitor to Tavistock should miss following the Town Trail and Drake's Walk which follows the towpath of the canal towards Drake's birthplace at Crowndale. The great man is commemorated in a bronze statue at the end of Plymouth road. The exact date of Francis Drake's birth is not certain, but it is thought to have been 1540. Little is known of his childhood or his early years at sea but Francis Drake did sail with Sir John Hawkins who was engaged in the Guinea trade. Not all of the enterprises of the two succeeded and Drake commanded the vessel *Judith* which was part of Hawkins's fleet to San Juan de Ulùa in 1567 which ended in failure. They had more success from three voyages to the West Indies between 1570 and 1572 and Drake and Hawkins were becoming rich. If truth be told they probably engaged in more than a little piracy and no Spanish vessel was safe from this pair of sea-dogs. Thus Francis Drake became popular with Queen Elizabeth, but he was no rival to Sir Walter Ralegh (about 1554–1616) who was as much a graceful courtier as a sailor and one who took care not to spend too long at sea. Drake on the other hand sailed long and often and was thus far enough removed from politics to be safe. In 1577 he set sail for the River Plate in the *Pelican*, which he later renamed the *Golden Hind*, with his route taking him through the Straits of Magellan, after which he sacked Valpariso before rounding the Cape of Good Hope and thus completing his circumnavigation of the world. When Drake arrived home in 1581 he was knighted by Queen Elizabeth I and it is of interest that Queen Elizabeth II used the same sword to Knight another West Countryman, Sir Francis

Chichester when he returned from his single handed round the world trip. Drake was a favourite of Elizabeth no doubt because of his bravery and sheer audacity. He also pleased her by destroying much Spanish armament in Cadiz Harbour in 1587 – the King of Spain's beard was said to be singed – but more to the point it delayed the Armada and gave the English time to prepare their defensive fleet. When the Armada came in 1588 Drake held the post of Vice Admiral and commanded one of the divisions of ships. The story of him finishing his game of bowls is probably true and not so foolish or conceited as it sounds. As a skilled seaman he knew well that the stiff wind blowing at the time would batter and weaken the enemy and confine his own ships in harbour for an hour or two. History records that the defeat of the Armada meant an immediate feeling of safety and euphoria in England. There is no doubt that the people felt that but the Queen and her politicians still had worries and Elizabeth must have blessed Drake again in 1589 when he and Sir John Norris attacked and plundered the port of Corûna and sank many ships. When Sir Francis Drake died in his 50s whilst still active he was denied well earned and honourable retirement but perhaps he would have preferred it that way. There are many reminders of his life in and around Plymouth and Tavistock and we look forward to the day when the local Tourist Authority establish a "Francis Drake Country" tour just as their colleagues in the north east have done for Captain Cook.

> My ladye hath a sable coach,
> With horses two and four
> My ladye hath a gaunt bloodhound
> That goeth on before.
> My lady's coach hath nodding plumes,
> The driver hath no head,
> My ladye is an ashen white,
> And one that long is dead.

We were reminded of this poem as we drove along the A30 into Okehampton at dawn on a misty December morning with icicles hanging from the walls and trees to produce a ghostly light. We had journeyed from Tavistock and the lady in the poem was Lady Howard of Tavistock who had a fearsome reputation. She certainly had four husbands and was said to have murdered all of them. Such an evil woman can surely not rest in peace and it is said that she travels every night from Fitzford near Tavistock to Okehampton Castle and taking the form of a black dog. Her task is to collect a blade of grass, but the legend does not tell us why.

Okehampton has rid itself of a more recent curse – modern traffic, which is now shunted around the town on the new A30 bypass. At one time Okehampton was a staging post on the Turnpike road leading from Cornwall, through Devon and onto London and many of the old inns still serve excellent bar snacks and are in a good state of repair. One old toll house still stands and is known as Bus House and there is an old river crossing at West Bridge on the original fording point across the Okement reservoir. The town's strategic position on the crossroads leading south east and south west has been vital since Celtic times as well as being an access point into Dartmoor. The Celts named the river the Okement which meant swift and noisy and this it certainly is at times of heavy rain and snowmelt. The Saxons built a hilltop settlement well above the flood levels and it is on this elevated spot that the church of All Saints was later built on the site of the fort of Ocmundtune. Following a disastrous fire in 1842, the church was largely rebuilt but the magnificent 16th century tower survived almost intact. There are sweeping views over the town from the church and also from the castle on the southern outskirts of the town and which still dominate the road into Cornwall.

Although ruined, the castle has retained all of its atmosphere, and the skillful landscaping by the builders is also still evident. The fortress stands over the steep wooded valley of River West Okement and was in its prime the largest castle in Devon built soon after the Norman Conquest to ensure that the native population remained subdued. The design of the castle indicates that the Normans still felt insecure and their raised motte was protected by both a barbican and a gatehouse whilst between them ran a long narrow passage almost resembling a maze and which would certainly have confused invaders. The great hall with its thick walls and a kitchen with two huge ovens also shows that the inhabitants would be well able to withstand a siege. The castle was largely dismantled during the

Okehampton Castle – a haunting ruin.

16th century, but a great deal remains including the Norman motte and also a substantial part of the keep. Now maintained by English Heritage the castle opens from Good Friday or April 1st whichever is earlier to the 30th September from 10 am to 6 pm. During the rest of the year it opens from Tuesday to Sunday from 10 am to 4 pm and there is an entry fee. This is one ruin which should not be rushed and we always make sure that we take our lunch to enjoy in the surrounding woodlands or down by the river in the well laid out picnic site. On a quiet June evening we watched the sun set, sipped a glass of wine, ate an apple pie smothered in rich Devon cream and listened to a tawny owl family calling to each other as adults carried food to the nest in a hollow birch. Beneath the tree we found a number of pellets which we gathered and later pulled them apart to discover that the owls had been feeding on bank vole, common shrew and long tailed field mice. This is one of the many places in Devon where it is possible to discover history and natural history within a very short distance.

In Okehampton itself on West Street is the Museum of Dartmoor Life which is sited in an old mill complete with a splendid waterwheel. There are craft and gift shops plus a Visitors' Centre and an adjacent tearoom. The museum is well signed from the A30 and there is plenty of free parking. The museum opens between 10 am and 5 pm from Monday to Saturday between March and December 20th and between June and September it also opens on Sundays. Here are displays of geology, pre-history, folklore and industries of the area including mining. This is an ideal place to plan a discovery of Dartmoor. The museum itself is housed in an historical building dating to 1811 when it was an agricultural mill and warehouse. Here is one of the famous Dartmoor letter boxes which contains a stamp with which visitors can frank their own postcards. Adjacent to the museum is a well stocked Information Centre. Okehampton itself, although now something of a tourist centre, still generates a substantial proportion of its income from farming with rich fields sandwiched between the valleys of four lovely rivers – Okement, Taw, Torridge and Lew. This agricultural dependence can be best appreciated by a visit to the Okehampton Show which takes place in August. This is an ideal area to spend a few days exploring before returning to the hustle and bustle of Exeter, heading towards the coastal resorts or Plymouth, or pushing up onto Dartmoor. To the south Dartmoor can be seen at its brooding best and its two highest peaks can be seen. These are Yes Tor and High Willhays both of which are above 2000 feet (609 metres) and therefore qualify as mountains.

There is a fine 3 mile drive along the valley of the Taw to Sticklepath where there is one of the finest industrial museums in Devon. The Museum of Waterpower at Finch Foundry has the same opening hours as the Museum of Dartmoor Life and the two should be discovered as a pair as they form a delightful contrast. Finch Foundry is a 19th century tool works with its machinery powered by three mighty waterwheels of primitive design, but of great and smooth efficiency. There is a cafe, gift shop and the free car park can be used as a base for a number of country walks. Between 1814 and 1960 the finest edged tools in the West Country were forged here and the place still throbs to the sound of steam hammer and rushing water – a real trip back into a byegone age.

There is one problem for those who wish to discover Dartmoor, especially if using Okehampton as a base and this relates to the activities of the Ministry of Defence. On days

The old steam hammers at Finch Foundry Sticklepath are real museum pieces.

when firing practices are taking place access is restricted and this annoys walkers. We can understand both sides of the argument. In an ideal situation we should all be able to walk wherever we wish, but farmers must grow crops, foresters preserve vital trees and our land must be protected by highly trained combatants. Neither must we forget that too many heavy-booted ramblers can cause a great deal of erosive damage and disturbance to wildlife. The latter is surprisingly resilient and adapts well to army manouvers and a compromise has been reached on Dartmoor. The soldiers fly a warning red flag and providing walkers keep a look out, a satisfactory compromise is reached.

Around Dartmoor

We have found that the local people are aware of firing times and most complaints come from less well informed and usually more belligerent visitors.

Before leaving the Okehampton area and turning our attention to central Dartmoor there are a few lovely little villages well worth discovering including Sampford Courtenay, North Tawton, Belstone and Northlew.

Few settlements are prettier than Sampford Courtenay with a colourful collection of cob and thatch cottages lining the main street and set on the A3072. In a depression close to the Hole Brook, a tributary of the Okement, is a granite church of St. Andrew which for a brief period in 1549 became the focus of English ecclesiastical history. At that time Henry VIII had not overcome the problems separating his new Church of England from the grip of Rome and the new prayer book was not willingly accepted in many areas. In 1549 Henry was dead and those who governed for the new and very sickly 12 year old King, especially the Earl of Somerset, feared the Catholics led by the example of the future Queen Mary would restore the mass once Edward VI died. The villagers of Sampford Courtenay refused to use the new prayer book and burned it whilst insisting that the Whitsuntide Mass was conducted in Latin. The local magistrates led by William Hellyons decided that they could not allow their influence to be usurped and converged on the village. Such were the feelings aroused that a battle ensued, Hellyons was hacked to death by farmers armed with billhooks and they then marched off to express their fears to the authorities in Exeter. Their efforts fell on deaf ears and on 17th August 1549 the ill-equipped and badly led farmers were defeated in battle and very few returned to their native village. Just north of Sampford Courteney is another pretty hamlet with the most attractive name of Honeychurch. This name does not derive from the product of the bee but from the Saxon, Hunna who owned the land. With the coming of the Normans the manor was given to Walter who apparently was able to farm the land using the slave labour of four serfs. At this time the Saxon church was replaced by a Norman structure. Much of this early Norman building survives although it was added to and changed during the 15th century when a tower and an attractive south porch were built. Despite these additions

Honeychurch is the smallest church in this area of Devon. On the north wall there is a large painting of the coat of arms of Elizabeth Ist. This was probably added following the Queen's restoration of the Church of England following the death of her Catholic sister Mary and the people of Honeychurch, unlike their neighbours at Sampford Courtenay, were pleased to return to the English prayer book. Could there have been real conflict between the two in 1549? Alas we shall never know.

North Tawton should perhaps be regarded as more of a town than a village and had a market charter as early as 1199 and remained important until the 18th century when its wool trade began to decline. This area also had a period of religious conflict but this time it was John Wesley who suffered. When he arrived at North Tawton in 1765 to preach his version of the Gospel the local clergy persuaded their congregation to set a pack of dogs on Wesley and those unwise enough to visit the town square to listen to his words. These days the square is dominated by a clock set up in 1877 to celebrate Queen Victoria's Jubilee and this stands in front of the market hall constructed in 1849 probably to try to persuade customers that the wool market was not dead. Another reminder of the good old days and situated close to the town is the last of the woollen mills to survive on the banks of the Taw. The Broad Hall with its mullioned windows dates to 1680 and also relates to the days when Devon wool ruled North Tawton.

Just a few miles north-west of Okehampton is Northlew, close to which is Milland Farm which is a working museum which is open from April to October and from Tuesday to Friday. There is a craft workshop plus a collection of rare breeds of sheep. Also at Northlew is the Lambretta Collection including vintage scooters, three-wheelers, tractors and a wide selection of now rare die cast toys.

The whole of the countryside around Okehampton is a delight and it would take years to discover every nook and cranny. Whenever we have to return to Exeter we regret leaving Okehampton, but we always know that it will not be long before we return and if the weather is right we can journey through the very heart of Dartmoor.

CHAPTER 4
Inside Dartmoor

Dartmoor itself is the highest and largest stretch of land in the south west of England, a wild, bleak area of granite tors and with a rich and fascinating literary history not least among which is the notorious *Hound of the Baskervilles*. The area needed some measure of protection in 1951 when 365 square miles (945 square kilometers) were designated Britain's fourth National Park and included within it is an ancient Royal Forest. As we saw in the last chapter extensive areas to the north are now used as military areas and firing ranges with access to many of these often restricted. There are several settlements within and around the moor which can be used as bases from which to discover the area including those mentioned in the last chapter plus Bovey Tracey, Moretonhampstead, Chagford, Widecombe-in-the-Moor, Postbridge and Princetown.

Bovey Tracey should be the first place on the discoverers' list because it is the headquarters of the Dartmoor National Park. Its grounds, partly occupied by a Rare Breeds Farm, is an exciting place to visit during its opening period throughout the summer. For those who prefer wildlife then Bovey Tracey is the base for a good number of woodland and riverside walks. Nearby are Shaptor and Furzeleigh woods which are in the Wray valley and are administered by the Woodland Trust. There are also nature trails among the private estate of around 50 acres (20 hectares) which make up Becky Falls near Manaton. This is one of Dartmoor's most attractive areas and there is an entry fee for each car. This allows well supervised parking and access to a licenced restaurant and tea room, a gift and craft shop, picnic areas and toilets. The central attraction is the 70 feet (21.3 metres) waterfall reached along a footpath through magnificent woodlands and a stream spanned by bridges. The Victorians loved these woods and so do we. Here live fox, badger, otter, stoat, weasel and long tailed field mouse whilst flowers include primrose, bluebell, wood sorrel, dog violet and many other species. The area is open daily from 10 am to

6 pm between Easter and November. It has been popular since 1866 when the railway line was opened and ferried tourists to Moretonhampstead and in the 1930s a regular shuttle service brought tourists from the station at Lustleigh. Although the rail link has long been closed there is still a flow of walkers across Bovey Brook and through Hound Tor Woods to the falls.

Manaton itself is an attractive village and so is nearby Lustleigh. Second home speculators have reduced some of the 'lived-in' quality of the villages. Close to Manaton's mainly 15th century parish church, dedicated to St. Winifred, is Wingstone Farm which was the home of John Galsworthy between 1904 and 1924. Born in 1867 and educated at Harrow and New College Oxford, Galsworthy trained for the law, but influenced by his cousin's wife with whom he was living and later married, he became a writer. After a few minor excursions into novels he produced in 1904, a series of stories under the title *Man of Devon* and here is the first mention of the Forsyte family whose sagas have become a part of literary and television history. John Galsworthy died in 1933 and his biography was published by C. Dupré in 1976. Manaton must have been an inspirational place to write with its church close to a peaceful village green. The interior of the church is rightly famous for a delightfully carved screen. The scene here can have changed little since literary giants such as Conrad, Garnett, Bernard Shaw and the naturalist W. H. Hudson visited Galsworthy and walked with him up onto the moor. No doubt they all visited and marvelled at Bowerman's Nose, a huge pillar of exposed granite which looks almost as if it was man made or a single stone left over from a Bronze Age circle. The walk past Bowerman's Nose leads onto Hound Tor and the pinnacle-like structure of Greator Rocks. In 1961 an ancient village was excavated in this area and which may have had its origins in Saxon times. Nine houses and three barns were found which were apparently abandoned when the Black Death struck towards the end of the 14th century. This is wonderful country always breezy, and with the air vibrating to the sound of lark, lapwing and pipit.

Just to the north west of the village of Lustleigh are a number of fine walks around Kennick, Tottiford and Trenchford reservoirs which are sheltered by conifer plantations. Lustleigh itself is dominated by a huddle of thatched shops, cafes and

The thatched village of Lustleigh is one of the most beautiful in Britain.

cottages and a pretty church. The Cleave Inn is another fine thatched building dating to the 15th century whilst above is the scenic Lustleigh Cleave from which can be seen the River Bovey. Despite what can best be described as an insensitive 19th century restoration some gems were left in the church including effiges of medieval knights and their ladies in the south trancept and north aisle and also retained was the ornately carved screen dating to the reign of Bloody Mary Tudor (1553–1558).

After exploring these valleys and before proceeding to Moretonhampstead we always return to Bovey Tracey, an ancient market town which has long described itself as the gateway to Dartmoor and which has been settled at least since Saxon times. It developed because of an important crossing point of the River Bovey. Following the Norman conquest the manor was given to the de Tracy family who came from Traci close to Bayeux. The family had one infamous member, one Sir William who was implicated in the murder of Thomas à Becket in Canterbury Cathedral in 1170. Sir William Tracy may have tried to make amends for his sin by endowing a church dedicated to St. Thomas but this burned down and was replaced by a more substantial church with a 14th century tower, a richly carved screen, some wonderfully carved misericords and a stone pulpit. The real joy is the screen which was one of the gifts of Lady Margaret Beaufort, Countess of Richmond who owned the manor. Bovey Tracey would have been a most important place during this period as this lady was the mother of the man who defeated Richard III on Bosworth Field in 1485 and became Henry VII, the founder of the Tudor dynasty.

The de Tracey lands were at Parke close to the 17th century bridge over the Bovey and the original manor house was demolished in 1826 and replaced by the present building which is now owned by the National Trust and which, as mentioned earlier in this chapter, is leased to the National Park as its headquarters. In the complex are interpretive displays of all aspects of the moor and it was here we learned that Bovey Tracey's early fortune was not based upon wool but upon ball clay. A substantial pottery was established in 1772 and at its prime was the most important in the west of England. Three bottle shaped kilns still stand on Pottery Road now part of a modern industrial estate.

From Bovey Tracey there are beautiful views of Dartmoor and especially towards Haytor. It is worth the effort to enjoy the view from Haytor Rocks which are 1,490 feet (453.9 metres) above sea level. Many think that Haytor is the most dramatic of all the tors which stand out from the peaty grasslands which surround it. On a good day the paths leading to Haytor are crowded with visitors and pony treckers are also a feature of the area. Quarrying once went on around the twin peaks of Haytor particularly in the early 19th century when George Templer had a horse-drawn railtrack constructed and the line of this can still be traced in parts. Haytor granite was much in demand and used for the pillars of the British Museum, the National Gallery and for the arches of London Bridge. This was bought by an American and transported block by block to Arizona where it now spans the Colorado. Nearby is the ruined engine house and the shaft of an old copper mine from which 2300 tons of copper were extracted between 1858 and 1867. If the weather is poor on Haytor then a visit to the nearby National Nature Reserve at Yarner Wood will provide plenty of shelter. Nature trails push through the wood and descriptive leaflets are on sale

The Alms Houses at Moretonhampstead.

but because of the delicate balance of the ecology a permit is needed to move off the trails. The 375 acres (150 hectares) of woodland are dominated by oak with birch being common in areas of disused farmland but some conifers have been planted and there are also areas of open moorland. This is a favoured reserve for those in search of butterflies for here are found the rare white admiral and the holly blue. Birds also occur in greater density than in the more exposed areas of Dartmoor and on a May morning we watched woodcock displaying and listened to the song of redstart, pied flycatcher, which have been encouraged by the provision of nesting boxes, and wood warbler. Parts of Yarner Wood and also Lustleigh Cleave are so damp that liverworts, mosses and ferns both common and rare species thrive and some areas are dominated by the pretty yellow-green flowers of golden saxifrage which can be found early in March in some sheltered spots.

Moretonhampstead is an ideal route to Dartmoor for those approaching from the east and the tower of its church set on a hill can be seen from some distance. Actually the whole town is set on a hillside. The two main thoroughfares are Cross Street and Fore Street, both of which are lined with pleasant cottages leading down to a system of fields and hedgerows. Behind these are the rolling hills of Dartmoor. This has been a busy little spot since the 13th century when it was at the heart of

Devon's developing woollen industry with power coming from the rushing streams which flowed very reliably off Dartmoor. Here were fullers and tuckers, tanners, ropers, candlers and paper-makers. Moretonhampstead at this time must have been a rich place with its prosperity reflected in its buildings but alas a disastrous fire in 1845 destroyed the majority of these. A set of colonnaded almshouses built in 1637 have survived, as has the splendid church dating mainly to the 15th century and in its time was richly endowed by those who made their fortunes from the woollen industry. The almshouses are owned by the National Trust but are not open to the public. Below the church and close to the Alms Houses is the Cross Tree, with both the cross and the tree still in fine condition.

Three miles west of Moretonhampstead on the Princetown road is the Miniature Pony Centre which is open daily from early March to 31st October between 10 am and 5 pm. Here is situated the Kerswell Stud of miniature ponies, and the centre claims to have the largest herd of these delightful creatures to be found anywhere in the world. There are also other breeds of horses including palominos. Other miniature animals on view are prize-winning Dexter cows, pygmy goats, Shetland sheep, dwarf rabbits, bantams and some very rare miniature donkeys. This is a 'hands on' centre and children and photographers have a field day. There is a traditional stable yard and farm buildings which are the homes of the ponies, some of which can be ridden by the children during the day. Overlooking a system of pretty lakes is a restaurant serving home-made food, morning coffee and Devon cream teas. There is a picnic area and a very well stocked gift shop. No dogs are allowed into the centre but guide dogs are allowed and kennels are provided for other dogs which owners may not wish to leave in their cars.

Two interesting villages within range of Moretonhampstead are Christow and Bridford and both have magnificent countryside within a mile or so of their centres. Close to Christow is Canonteign Country Park whilst Bridford has some fine woodlands sandwiched between Chagford and the village. Mining was a vital industry around Christow with copper, lead, silver and manganese obtained in economic quantities. Of the parish church little remains of the original 15th century building with the sturdy granite tower dating to 1630 and the

At the Miniature Pony Centre Moretonhampstead.

chancel rebuilt in 1862. Inside is a memorial to the life of Edward Pellew (1757–1833) whose military career and bravery in North Africa gained him fame and led to his becoming Viscount Exmouth. He built Canonteign House in 1828 close to a site occupied by a Tudor manor house which he purchased from the Davy family in 1812. The old house, restored in the 1970s stands close to disused mines and is known as Canonteign Barton. The system of streams and waterfalls which now form the basis of the Country Park provided water to wash the ores from the mines until the last extraction of copper in the 1880s. The most dramatic of the waterfalls is now named after Lady Exmouth and tumbles down almost 230 feet (70.7

Visitors inspecting the rosettes won by the miniature ponies at Moretonhampstead.

metres) before breaking over rocks in the woodland glen and spraying white water and spray in all directions. We once visited the area in a heaving rainstorm in late July and the noise of Lady Exmouth was truly awe-inspiring. The watercourses are the breeding grounds of dipper, grey wagtail and common sandpiper whilst in the woods breed buzzard, sparrowhawk, greater spotted woodpecker, treecreeper and redstart.

Bridford was also a wealthy mining centre concentrating on the production of lead. It has a parish church dating to the 14th century and some excellently carved stalls and bench ends but even these are overshadowed by the rood screen funded for his church by Walter Southcote who was rector between 1508 and 1550. What a pity that the Reformation destroyed so many rood screens of the parish churches of England, but how grateful we must be that some, like this fine example at Bridford, remain. Bridford Woods are extensive and reach almost to Chagford, but we never rush away from this area, kept in fine condition by the National Trust, and we always allow a whole day to discover the variety of wildlife, and to explore the hamlets of Dunsford, Prestonbury Castle and Fingle Bridge. The glory of these woods are the wild daffodils which are dominant in early spring and had Wordsworth been a Devon lad he would have written of their sprightly dance in Bridford woods instead of on the banks of Ullswater in his native Cumbria. The woodlands line the valley of the River Teign which rises on Dartmoor and flows on to Chagford, Lower Ashton, collecting the waters of the Bovey close to Bovey Tracey and then on to sea at Teignmouth beyond Newton Abbot. Our favourite stretch of the Teign is on the linear track through Bridford Woods. Otters are occasionally seen here. Water voles are also common, a sure sign that the Teign is an unpolluted stream. This pretty rodent – Ratty of the *Wind in the Willows* – is a vegetarian which is very clean and fastidious in its habits. Some naturalists have suggested that the entry hole to its underground nest is so narrow that the vole has to squeeze into it and thus 'iron out' any excess water on its coat! Wood anemones, bluebells and primroses also grow in profusion in Dunsford Wood.

Dunsford is yet another beautiful village with cottages of thatch and cob and from which a mosaic path of pebbles leads up to the church which stands high over the Teign. Inside the church is a monument to the worthy Sir Thomas Fulford the High Admiral of England who died in 1610 and is depicted with his wife and seven children. Sir Thomas lived at nearby Great Fulford and his ancestors settled the area from the reign of Richard I (1189–1199). Of even older origin are Cranbrook Castle and Prestonbury Castle which are the remains of Iron Age forts. Prestonbury is very well preserved and overlooks one of Dartmoor's most famous beauty spots at Fingle Bridge. This was constructed of granite during the 16th century to carry the packhorse traffic but all it carries these days is a stream of summer tourists commuting between the riverside paths on one side of the Teign with the hotel and shop on the other.

A more modern building is Castle Drogo, which is only two miles to the east of Chagford. The house was built during the early years of the 20th century on a rocky crag overlooking the Teign valley. It was built for the Drewe family to the ingenious design of Sir Edwin Lutyens which catered for the families modern needs including their own hydro-electric and telephone systems, as well as providing the feel and looks of a solid medieval castle. It was built mainly of granite and

Fingle Bridge is one of Devon's most attractive packhorse bridges.

was completed just before the Second World War. It is open daily from 11 am to 6 pm between April and October and is in the care of the National Trust. There is a formal rose garden, impressive yew hedges, a croquet lawn, a restaurant and a shop.

  Chagford is certainly an ancient settlement but historians are not agreed on the precise period of its establishment although there were certainly pre-historic settlements around the area. The name itself is Saxon and means Gorse-Ford, although the settlement has had a variety of names including Chaggesford, Chegford, Chageford and Kageford. At the time of Domesday five local manors were listed including Scapelie (Shapley), Midelcote (Middlecott), Risford (Rushford), Taincombe (Teigncombe) and of course Chagford. As industry developed on Dartmoor, Chagford played an increasingly important role. In 1305 it was granted the status of a Stannary town which meant that it collected tin mined locally and assessed it for taxation purposes. Soon Chagford was handling 40% of Devon's tin and it remained the most important Stannary town until well into the 15th century. Even after that Chagford remained important even if it was not dominant. It is, however, certainly an ideal place to begin the study of Dartmoor tin and the countryside around the town is full of reminders of the industry. Trial pits can be seen on Nattadon Hill, traces of once functional workings are situated at Bushdown and West Vitifer, whilst historians have identified 16th century workings around Broomhill.

Apart from mining Chagford enjoyed a period of prosperity due to the woollen industry and this has also left its mark following a decline after reaching a peak of activity in the early 19th century. Agriculture, however, has continued to play a vital rôle in the local economy, but in recent years another industry has become important – tourism.

The hub of Chagford is still the Square dominated by the one-time Market House, octagonal in shape and built in 1862 on the site of the old butchers' shambles. At the same time the Victorians swept away most of the thatched inns, shops and cottages around the square and replaced them with more functional but surprisingly attractive buildings. A market is no longer held in the Square and the octagonal house after use as a lock-up and an armoury for the local volunteers now functions as a bus shelter, shops, toilets and a community police office. It still bears, however, the old Toll Board showing the cost of pitching a stall or bringing livestock or goods to market. A cow and a calf cost 3d and a cart of cheese 2d – for those who cannot remember the pre-decimalisation 12d made one shilling and this was equivalent to 5 pence. Although there is no market the Square is still busy and there are several attractive shops including two ironmongers at the top of the square next door to each other. Both of these have been owned by Chagford families for many years and they live in friendly and peaceful co-existence. Both are old time shops and we walked around James Bowden and Son and Webber and Sons with a notebook in which we listed what was on sale. Nobody asked what we were doing and nobody tried the hard sell, although both shops were helpful as we made one or two holiday purchases. Our list of goods on offer included cameras, cutlery, clothes and china, fishing rods, film and garden forks, saddles and soap, pet food, paint and permits to fish and an assortment of footwear. The shops not only look good but they also smell like old shops ought to smell. They have what hypermarkets will never have – history and atmosphere. Do

Chagford Market House dominating the square of the Town.

not leave Chagford without buying a memento from each of the shops.

Two pubs around or close to the Square are worthy of note namely the Ring O'Bells and the Three Crowns. The locals abbreviate the Ring O'Bells to the Ringers and a look at the exterior reveals the evidence of past alterations. At one time an external staircase led up to a substantial doorway which has now been converted into a window. This was once the entrance to a room used for important functions such as meetings and dinners and it also served occasionally as a coroner's court. The

Three Crowns built in the 16th century as a Manor House by Sir John Widdon has a much more grizzly history. Here in 1643 died Sidney Godolphin, famous as a Cavalier and as a poet. Some have suggested that he was shot in the porch of the building but others believe that he was wounded in a skirmish and was carried to the house where he died. A plaque in the porch records this sad event and although Chagford did not play a major rôle in the Civil War its residents did come to blows with those of Moretonhampstead who were fiercely for the Roundheads whilst the Chagfordians were solidly behind the King. There was another tragic event associated with the Three Crowns building – it is said Mary Whiddon was shot as she was being married at St. Michael's church in 1641 and that R. D. Blackmore used this event as the inspiration for a scene in his novel *Lorna Doone*. This was described in full in our companion volume *Discovering Exmoor and North Devon*. Mary Whiddon is commemorated by an inscription on the floor of the sanctuary which reads 'Here lieth Mary the daughter of Oliver Whiddon Esquire who died on the 11th day of October Ano Dom 1641.'

> 'Reader wouldst know who here is laid,
> Behold a matron yet a maid
> A modest look, a pious heart,
> A Mary for the better part.
> But dry thine eyes why wilt thou weep,
> Such maidens do not die but sleep.'

St. Michael's church is fully described in an admirable little leaflet available from a table just inside the door. It was dedicated on July 30th 1261 by Bishop Branscombe who founded many West Country churches. Chagford must have been high on the Bishop's list because, as we have seen, it was then an important and expanding town. Some 13th century work still remains, but the present church dates mainly to the 15th century with the Lady Chapel added in 1482. Historians believe that there was a Christian settlement at Chagford much earlier and possibly in Saxon times as it is only about 12 miles from Crediton which was then the centre of early Christianity in Devon. Crediton is also described in our volume *Discovering Exmoor and North Devon*. Until 1975 an ancient oak stood just

Wild Dartmoor ponies grazing close to Fenworthy Forest.

outside the south wall of the church and was known as the Cross Tree. This was felled as it was obviously unsafe but it may have been the ancestor of a holy tree which grew on the site long before a stone church was constructed. We wonder if another oak should be planted or are we being too sentimental?

The church itself is best described as a solid granite building in the Perpendicular style. Inside on the church roof bosses can be seen the carving of three conjoint rabbits, a sign of the tinners and there is evidence to show that Chagford's churchwardens had substantial mining investments. The three rabbits carved for the tinners had to share only three ears! There are also many original features within the church and of particular note is the parclose screen. There is also a sanctuary door knocker which those being pursued could grasp and at least gain breathing space. A piece of history which has been lost for ever were the wall paintings which were typical of medieval churches. In 1551 during the reign of Edward VI the son of Henry VIII, anti-Catholic opinions were running high and many church paintings including those at Chagford were defaced or painted over. During a restoration of 1857 the surfaces of walls, arches and pillars were scraped clean and the pictures destroyed. In the context of the time this action made sense but with the modern techniques available it would have been possible to work wonders on the paintings but alas they have gone for ever.

Just to the south west of Chagford is Fenworthy Forest and Reservoir from which issues the South Teign river which joins the North Teign just before Chagford. The coniferous plantation and the forest have swamped some of Dartmoor's most ancient settlements. This would not be allowed to happen in these days when some semblance of a conservation conscience is developing, but all that can be done at Fenworthy is to minimise the damage. Having said that there is still much to discover and on a good day the area is idyllic. When Fenworthy reservoir was constructed it was allowed to flood a Stone Age village, a venerable old manor house and a bridge plus all linking roads vanished beneath the water. We love to follow the forest walks and listen to the goldcrests singing their high pitched notes, but it is not just the birds of the conifers which are worth searching for because clearings have been left free of trees and in these are a number of hut circles and one stone circle. On the bare hillside above the plantation to the west are a pair of stone circles known as the Grey Wethers, so named because from a distance they can look like a ring of resting sheep. They look in surprisingly good order but this is because they were 'imaginatively restored' in the early 1900s by Sabine Baring-Gould who had the stones dug out of the grass and supported on blocks of granite brought up onto the moor for this express purpose. We once sat close to the Grey Wethers and watched a wheatear carrying food to its young whilst listening to a male cuckoo advertising his presence.

The North Teign river is also a rich area for stone circles, settlements and cairns, especially around Gidleigh. From Chagford the road to Gidleigh crosses the Teign by a packhorse bridge which is probably 16th century, the village itself being dominated by a venerable old beech tree. There has been a church here at least since Domesday but the present building is mainly 15th century. The manor derived its name from the Saxon Gydda who was the mother of Harold Godwinson, a lady who sought refuge in her West Country estates following her son's defeat by William the Norman at Hastings. Gradually her influence and estates were usurped by the Conqueror. Dartmoor is full of old bridges and there is a clapper bridge spanning a stream, which cuts through the churchyard. Nearby is another remnant of Saxon England with a ruin of a typical long house and the leet of a very ancient mill. The Normans built a castle on the site but this was replaced in 1324 by the fortified manor house built for Sir William de Prouze. This too is now a ruin but the adjacent Tudor House has fared better having been restored in recent times. It was once a restaurant and is not now open to the public. Gidleigh is not well publicised and is therefore usually quiet.

This is certainly not the case with Widecombe-in-the-Moor.

Widdecombe, one of the most atmospheric villages on Dartmoor. This photograph was taken about 1926.

Tom Pearce, Tom Pearce, lend me your grey mare,
All along, down along, out along lee.
For I want to go to Widecombe Fair,
Wi' Bill Brewer, Jan Stewer, Peter Gurney,
Peter Davy, Dan'l Whiddon, Harry Hawk,
Old Uncle Tom Cobley and all,
Old Uncle Tom Cobley and all.

Inside Dartmoor

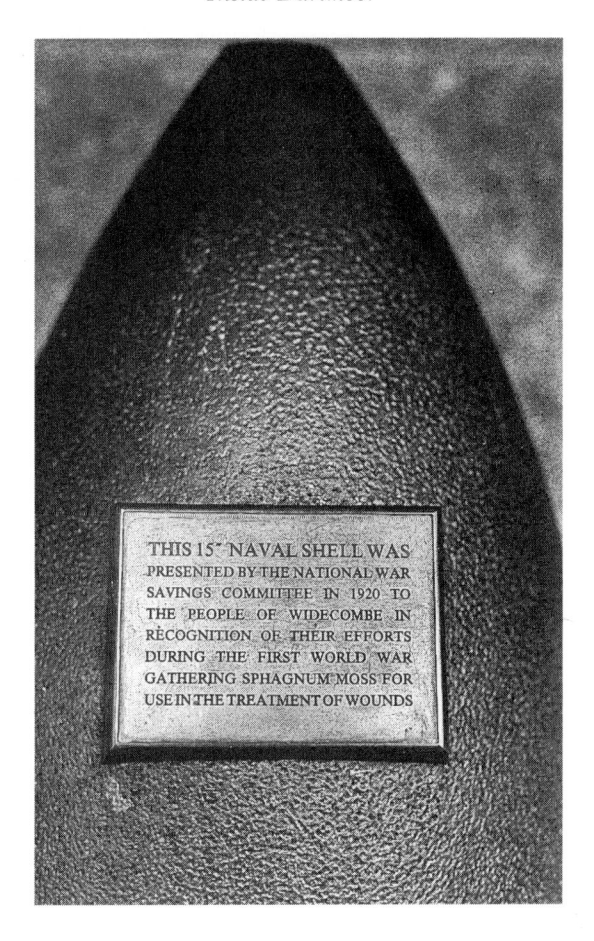

> THIS 15" NAVAL SHELL WAS
> PRESENTED BY THE NATIONAL WAR
> SAVINGS COMMITTEE IN 1920 TO
> THE PEOPLE OF WIDECOMBE IN
> RECOGNITION OF THEIR EFFORTS
> DURING THE FIRST WORLD WAR
> GATHERING SPHAGNUM MOSS FOR
> USE IN THE TREATMENT OF WOUNDS

Widecombe Fair is still held on the second Tuesday in September. Uncle Tom Cobley died in the 1790s and the above song was written down about 1880.

Our last visit to Widecombe was on a cold foggy day in January when Dartmoor seemed gaunt and quiet – yet this village was open and full of tourists. No wonder that the car park is almost as large as the village itself. The parish is the second largest in Devon covering more than 10,000 acres (4000 hectares) but has a resident population of only around 600.

Postbridge, perhaps the most famous clapper bridge in England.

Most of the land is above 800 feet (244 metres) with the highest point being the 1,697 feet (518 metres) Hameldon Beacon. The surrounding hillsides are studded with Bronze Age hut circles, burial chambers and barrows and archeologists have proved that the hut circles at Foales Arrishes were still being used well into the Iron Age.

Widecombe is dominated by its church with its 120 foot (36.6 metre) tower topped by four dramatic pinnacles. In the 13th century the locals were granted permission to build their own church rather than have to undergo the strenuous walk to the 'parish of the manor' at Lydford. Much of the finance required for Widecombe's church which is dedicated to St. Pancras was provided by the tin miners. They were particularly generous in the 14th century and it earned its name 'The Cathedral of the Moors'. Even though they now had their own church many of the parishioners still had to travel long distances and around 1500 Church House was built to provide accommodation. Later the house was divided into almshouses and has also served its time as a Poor House and a school. The National Trust now own the building and have set up a shop selling the usual books and postcards. Outside the shop is a First World War shell given to the village and bearing a plaque to record the nation's gratitude for those who collected tons of sphagnum moss. This is so absorbent that it was ideal as a battle dressing, in a war which was infamous for the carnage of the trenches. Widecombe church had its own share of tragedy; on the 21st October 1638 when, during a service, lightning struck the tower and part crashed down through the roof. At the same time a fireball passed through the church and killed four people. Naturally in this superstitious area the devil was blamed for this tragic event. Perhaps even this is preferable to describing it as an act of God. There is a tradition that on his way to devastate Widecombe the devil stopped for a glass of beer at the Tavistock Inn at Poundsgate and as the drink flowed down his throat it boiled. There is still a burn mark on the bar top where Old Nick rested his glass.

Widecombe manages to absorb many coach tours and other visitors without being disturbed and it never seems to run out of cream teas. The central village green is best known as Butte Park which was once an area set out for the local archers to practise their skills. Apart from the church and Church House there are other fine old buildings overlooking the green. Although it has been much altered and was damaged by a fire in 1977 the Old Inn still lives up to its name and was founded as early as the 14th century. The Glebe House, now a gift shop, was built about 1500 on land rented from the church and it still has a huge open fireplace and a bread oven. Just beyond the Post Office is a Saxon well which is said never to run dry, but these days its water is not thought pure enough to drink. Nearby is the old Smithy which was used until 1950 when it was converted into a museum devoted to the once vital old craft which no village could afford to be without. From a modern tourist point of view Widecombe-in-the-Moor has everything.

Postbridge, almost in the centre of the moor, is another tourist trap especially those who prefer to do their discovering on foot. The village may have been named because the post road from Exeter into Cornwall crossed the ancient bridge. It was probably built in the 14th century of flat slabs of granite laid across solid stone piers and is thus a true clapper bridge. In 1675 the first road atlas to be produced in Britain described it as 'Post Stone Bridge of 3 arches', which spans the East Dart river.

Even the 'modern' bridge which by-passed it is a joy to look at. Just to the south west of the village is a gunpowder mill begun in 1844 by George Frean from Plymouth who chose the isolated site for obvious safety reasons. There was sufficient water to drive the machinery and also a reliable supply of customers who were blasting away at the Dartmoor rocks as a building boom overtook the Victorian age. The business of gunpowder production was very profitable until the 1890s when Nobel's discovery of dynamite made it largely obsolete. Still standing are the ruined dwellings of the workers and the work's manager and also the old ground level flue and chimney. Part of the complex is now a working pottery.

An even older reminder of Dartmoor life is to be found at Grimspound reached from Postbridge along the B3212 and is obvious from the road. There is a small parking area and footpaths lead up to the settlement. This is an excellent example of a Bronze Age shepherd settlement occupied between 1800 BC and 550 BC and huddled into the folds of Dartmoor. It has the well preserved remains of 24 huts within a stone compound. The positions of door lintels and stone sleeping shelves can still be detected. Grim was an alternative name for Woden, an Anglo-Saxon god. The atmosphere of Grimspound was well known to Sir Arthur Conan Doyle who used it as Dr. Watson's hiding place during the unravelling of the case of *The Hound of the Baskervilles*.

The area has a much more modern claim to grim notoriety – Dartmoor Prison at Princetown. The town grew as a direct result of Thomas Tyrwhitt's opportunism in offering his land as the site for a prison and making a fortune in the process. In 1803 when Britain was at war with Napoleon's France many prisoners of war were kept in overcrowded, stinking, damp and only just floating hulks at anchor in Plymouth harbour. Tyrwhitt suggested a purpose built prison which was completed in 1809 and in 1812 America declared war on Britain and the first batch of 250 New World prisoners arrived in April of 1813. Princetown Parish church which is dedicated to St. Michael and All Angels and stands proudly some 1,825 feet (460 metres) above sea level. It was built by French prisoners who were paid sixpence ($2\frac{1}{2}$p) per day and the first service was held on 2nd January 1814 although the structure was not finished.

Grimspound – used as a setting by Conan Doyle.

It was completed by the Americans, but Dartmoor was still a prison and not a very healthy prison at that and more than half of the inmates died. There is a big granite cross in the churchyard standing over the individually unmarked graves. Peace with the Americans was signed in 1814, but the prisoners could not go home due to the shortage of suitable ships. The prisoners mutinied and seven were shot dead. Eventually the men were transported home and Dartmoor prison remained empty, but its obvious uses were realised in 1852 when it was opened as a civil prison. There are other buildings of interest including the Prison Officers Mess which was built as a Royal Hunting Lodge for Queen Victoria. The Plume of Feathers Inn is the oldest building in Princetown but only dates to 1785 and was once an important coaching inn. It was a useful building at the time that the prison was under construction and is a regular haunt with the enthusiasts who visit the famous Dartmoor letter boxes. The Devil's Elbow was once called the Railway Inn which is misleading as the track was originally a horse drawn system which had its terminus here. The Stable Bar was once just that – the home of the railroad horses! Thomas Tyrwhitt himself had his house here at Tor Royal which he built in 1785 with money made from the production of flax. Here he entertained Royal guests and it was Thomas who planned the Princetown to Plymouth horse-drawn railway which was laid in 1823 to transport stone and which later operated with steam locomotives until the mid 1950s. Tyrwhitt named the new settlement Princetown after the Prince of Wales who later became George IV. Princetown may not be everyone's idea of a tourist centre but it can be used as a base to discover Two Bridges and Dartmeet.

Two Bridges lies just to the south of the junction of the Cowsic stream and the West Dart river. Where these meet is approximately the centre of Dartmoor and close to the east bank of the West Dart is the famous Wistman's Wood which thanks to the work of Oliver Rackham and his fellow students has been more carefully documented than any similar area in Britain. Owned by the Duchy of Cornwall and now an English Nature Council Reserve of 60 acres (24 hectares) is dominated by stunted oaks. These grow on boulder-strewn slopes encrusted by lichens and cushioned by succulent mosses. They are kept damp by a high rainfall and the thick mists typical of Dartmoor. Ferns such as common polypody and broad buckler also thrive in these conditions. Thousands of years ago with a changing climate and also affected by careless human hands, only two or three stretches of the wild woods remain. The oaks belong to a type described as Pedunculate *Quercus robur,* typified by bearing their acorns on stalks. The technical name for a stalk is a peduncle and this accounts for their common name. Growing in these conditions it is no wonder that the oaks are somewhat stunted and although many specimens are more than 500 years old they seldom exceed 25 feet (7.6 metres) in height and their shape is gnarled and twisted by centuries of battering by high winds.

Beneath the shelter of the oaks grows wavy hair grass, soft grass, wood sorrel, heath bedstraw, wood sage, English stonecrop and the rather uncommon white climbing corydalis.

Close to Two Bridges is Crockern Tor which rises to a height of 1,391 feet (424 metres) and has for centuries been known as Parliament Rock and it is said that from the reign of Edward I (1272–1307) until about 1750 the tin miners held their Stannary Court at this point. Tavistock, Plympton, Chagford and Ashburton each sent 24 delegates who worked out the

Dartmoor prison looking gaunt and forbidding in early morning sleet and fog.

mining laws which were ratified by the Lord Warden of the Stannaries. In time the delegates seem to have become softer and preferred to meet in each of the four towns in rotation rather than make the tiring journey to the exposed Crockern Tor Parliament.

Tors may be one typical aspect of Dartmoor but its rivers are also dramatic especially during rain or following snow-melt. Dartmeet is an ideal place from which to discover the upper reaches which flow from the north of the moor a distance of 46 miles to the sea on the coast of South Devon. The East Dart and West Dart have their headwaters only about a couple of miles apart, the former flowing through Postbridge and the latter through Two Bridges. At Dartmeet the East Dart flows through Badger's Holt and then unites with the West Dart before continuing to New Bridge, Holne and Buckfastleigh. We love Dartmeet at anytime except at the height of summer when it can be bursting at the seams with tourists and the B3357 road and the bridge which carries it across the river tends to become congested.

On the whole, however, Dartmoor handles its tourists with ease and the same is true of the area known as the South Hams which is described in the next chapter.

CHAPTER 5

South Hams

Whenever we sit in front of a winter's fire in our northern home we think of summer, sunshine, sea, sands and scones saturated with cream and jam. There is only one place to find all of these things and that is in Devon and the most fertile area of this succulent county is known as the South Hams. The ancient district occupies the southernmost tip of the county, is sandwiched between the Rivers Dart and Tamar and stretches from Dartmoor to the sea-caressed headland of Prawle Point. Since the reign of Aethelwulf in AD 846 the area has been known as South Hams with 'Hamma' being the Old English name for a sheltered area. It has always been sheltered as it is washed by warm waters of the Gulf stream which extends the warmer seasons of the year and holds winter at bay. This makes South Hams the perfect place for a winter or early spring break when the flowers come early and the woods and beaches can provide cosy picnic places when other parts of the country are still lagging their pipes.

There are several excellent places from which South Hams can be discovered and at which a variety of accommodation is on offer. These are Totnes, Dartmouth, Kingsbridge, Modbury and Malborough.

A Tuesday morning in high summer is our favourite time to visit Totnes. This is the day when the market traders take extra time to get ready for work and arrive dressed in full Elizabethan costume with their ruffs and velvet clothes blending beautifully with the half-timbered buildings. Totnes is recovering from an almost disastrous fire in 1990 and the expensive restoration work has succeeded in repairing most of the scars. This friendly town of around 7,000 people is a delight at any time but at the Tuesday market it positively beams with good will and between 9 am and 1 pm the 'Elizabethan' market has many charity stalls on the forecourt of the Civic Hall. Setting off each Tuesday from Vine Island at 2.30 pm an Elizabethan guide leads a tour of the old town.

Prehistoric man was present in this sheltered spot on the banks of the navigable River Dart and archeologists have found Roman tiles beneath its present streets. We prefer to discount the legend that the town itself was founded by Brutus the grandson of a Greek Trojan named Aeneas. The first written record of Totnes is in the 10th century when it had an established mint producing coins bearing the head of King Edgar. Alfred the Great had established four 'mint' towns in Devon and which were also there to provide resistance to the invading Danes. These were Lydford, Exeter, Barnstaple and Halwell. The latter is now just a small village to the south of Totnes which has long been dominated by its neighbour. When William of Normandy finally subdued the Saxons in Devon Totnes, along with many other Manors, was granted to a Breton by the name of Judhel. By 1088 Judhel of Totnes had constructed a castle and established a Benedictine priory. It seems that there was already some sort of Saxon defence work on this hilltop and the Normans adapted this and what remains is a text book example of a motte and bailey castle. Here is the largest Norman courtyard to be found anywhere in Britain and is a popular place with visitors many of whom bring picnics. It is open daily and carefully maintained by English Heritage. The views from the ramparts over the town and the Dart valley can only be described as panoramic and spectacular. In the holiday season there always seems to be a steady stream of visitors flowing up the winding path to the castle, but when there is a Norman Festival the stream becomes a deluge of those in search of colourful archers and formidable looking mounted and armoured knights, the battle tanks of their age.

Judhel's job was to subdue the Saxons and his fortifications were constructed in a hurry. Once his successors had a relatively peaceful environment in which to live they could give more time to the production of a more solid and comfortable abode and in 1219 much of the original timber works were replaced by stone and in 1326 the circular keep of red sandstone was added. This and the ramparts are by far the best places to begin a study of the medieval town with stout walls and rounded corners. Originally the town had three gates of which the north and especially the east gate remain, the latter now happily restored following the fire. Usually referred to as the Arch, this Totnes

Totnes castle and church photographed from the Steamer Quay.

landmark now looks magnificent after having substantial sums of money spent upon it. Thus protected by its castle and walls Totnes became an important town and as it sent a member of Parliament to London it can regard itself as the second oldest borough in England after Colchester in Essex. In 1359 a Mayor was appointed and the splendid induction ceremony is continued to the present day, having been re-established in 1977.

Such a successful town, enclosed within the narrow confines of stout ramparts, was bound to run out of space and new houses were built on the western slopes leading down to the river. For some reason Totnes does not seem to have kept pace with Exeter and Ashburton which became rich on the profits of the 17th and 18th century serge industry. For this modern day discoverers should be pleased as few towns can rival Totnes as a medieval market centre. The town settled back into a time warp but continued to earn a living from slate quarrying which had begun in 1180 when many were shipped out to Winchester to roof its castle. Other industries, however, declined. Totnes built ships on the banks of the river and had a flourishing trade in exporting salted meat and fish especially pilchards but eventually Dartmouth harbour took over the rôle as the major port of the river.

Alas the old Benedictine Priory was demolished just after the Dissolution of monastic institutions on the orders of Henry VIII in the 1530s. Little of this building remains as the Guildhall was constructed on the site. This is open from Easter to the end of September from Monday to Friday. The hours of opening are 10 am to 1 pm and 2 pm to 5 pm. The town guide does not exaggerate when it describes the Guildhall as the most atmospheric building in Totnes. The town council still meet here and each of the more than 600 mayors since the 14th century has his (or her) name recorded for posterity in gold leaf. The building was granted to the town in 1553 by King Edward VI and the local folk were allowed to build their hall within the original walls of the 11th century priory and modern day photographers are drawn to the place and to the nearby Rampart Walk. Inside the building there are fascinating carvings, plasterwork from the Elizabethan period, plus a collection of Saxon coins minted at Totnes. There is also the public gallery from which trials could be observed and beneath the court is a cramped cell where wrong-doers were kept.

The Parish church situated close to the Guildhall is dedicated to St. Mary and is mainly 15th century. Its most famous feature is a rood screen delicately carved from Beer stone. The church reflects the prosperity of 15th century Totnes and its massive tower is clearly visible from the outskirts of the town. No expense was spared and around 1450 the builders were sent off around the country to inspect the best church towers and they no doubt had firm instructions to improve upon them. Money had to be found and the Bishop of Exeter played his part by granting indulgencies to all who made donations towards the construction of the red sandstone building, which dates mainly to the period between 1400 and 1460. Money, ambition and expertise all combined to produce a magnificent tower which was a sort of medieval ecclesiastical equivalent of 'keeping up with the Jones's'. Many Devon towers are typified by having a stair turret which can be seen projecting from the middle of one side usually at the south. There is a great similarity between Totnes tower and the one at Ashburton but the latter has its stair turret built into the northern face. Other features of St. Mary's are the beautiful Corporation pew fronts which were carved from wood in the 16th century and also a rather fine monument to the life of Christopher Blackhall a prominent merchant who died in 1633. The history of a town can usually be read within and around its church, but the discoverer should always allow plenty of time to explore all the available museums. Totnes is well endowed in the latter respect, having a number of excellent museums plus an attractive Information Centre sandwiched between two pillared porches situated at the Plains.

Totnes Museum has been described as an attractive gateway to the past – it is to us rather more than this and is one of our favourite places in the whole of Devon. It is housed in an Elizabethan Merchant's House on Fore Street and was built in 1575. It is open from April to October from Monday to Friday between 10.30 am and 1 pm and 2 pm to 5 pm. It also opens on Bank Holidays. This is not a dry academic place but a "hands on" informative exhibition aimed accurately at families. There is a display of pre-historic artefacts but quite rightly in this particular building there is heavy emphasis on the Elizabethan Age. The Victorian Age is also well represented and there is a very authentic looking grocer's shop of this period. Here are old adverts for Nestlés chocolate, McVities biscuits, Oxo, Pears and Sunlight soap, Cherry blossom boot polish and Birds custard powder. These days we live in a plastic age with highly coloured individual wrappings. The Victorians were also aware of presentation and they packaged their goods in beautiful enamelled tins. Some of these are now worth a small fortune. The Totnes Elizabethan Museum also remembers two of its most famous sons, William Wills and Charles Babbage. Wills was very famous in his day as an explorer of the Australian outback and who died there in 1861. He is better known in Australia than he is in Britain. There is a stone memorial to the explorer on the Plains not far from the Information Centre. In his short life (1843–1861) he achieved fame for crossing the Australian continent with the explorer Burke but John Wills died on the return journey.

Charles Babbage built a prototype computer in the 1820s and anticipated the Modern Age by around 150 years. The exhibition of his work in the museum proves beyond doubt that had it not been for those with vested interests working against him Babbage would have revolutionised science and mathematics. Another man of Totnes who deserves to be remembered is Nicholas Ball whose house is now occupied by Barclay's Bank which was built in 1585 and still has its magnificent frontage and a plaster ceiling gracing the first floor. Ball made his fortune from the Totnes pilchard fishery and when he died his wife Anne married Sir Thomas Bodley. It was eventually the pilchard money which funded the world famous Bodleian Library at the University of Oxford.

Bowden House Museum opens from Easter to September on Tuesday, Wednesday and Thursday and also on Bank Holiday Sundays and Mondays. The museum opens at 11 am, film shows are given at 1.30 pm and there are guided tours at 2 pm, 3 pm and 4 pm. These are guided tours with a difference as the family who run the museum dress up in Georgian costume. The house is part Tudor, part Queen Anne and has been beautifully restored. Here are collections of antique furniture, weapons and pictures and the house is also the site of the British Photographic Museum, having a huge collection of vintage cameras. There is a licenced cafe and children under 10 are admitted free of charge. Car boot sales are often held on Sundays in the car park.

The guides at Bowden House create the feeling of Georgian England and prepare the visitor for a trip to the Devonshire Collection of Period Costume on the High Street and displayed in one of Totnes's finest Tudor houses which once belonged to a rich merchant. It is open from the Spring Bank Holiday to the end of September from Monday to Friday 11 am to 5 pm and on Sunday from 2 pm to 5 pm.

Like many medieval towns Totnes relied heavily upon its river which was tidal and easily navigable and thus was crucial to its prosperity. The present bridge was built in 1828 to a design by Charles Fowler the designer of London's Covent Garden market and it leads to Bridgetown, the Steamer Quay, a pleasant park on Vire Island and a gentle Riverside Walk. During the season a blacksmith can be seen working a forge which has operated for more than 600 years and behind this is a prison cell. The two buildings were often situated close together as it was the blacksmith who forged the prisoners' chains. The Totnes Motor Museum is situated in a restored warehouse on the Steamer Quay. It is open each day from Easter to October from 10 am to 5.30 pm and houses a famous collection of vintage cars and a vast array of memorabilia. Totnes Quay was a busy harbour at the time of the Spanish Armada and in 1988 the town celebrated the 400th anniversary of its defeat. Local boats were made to look like warships and the glory days of Elizabethan England were re-enacted. On Steamer Quay there is a play galleon on which children can learn their history by the modern 'hands on' technique. This is still a busy place between April and October when there are daily trips to Dartmouth but the times vary according to the tide. All the cruise boats have tea, coffee and alcoholic bars, toilets and plenty of cover in case of bad weather. It is no idle boast to suggest that the 10 mile cruise down the river to Dartmouth is a real rival to those on the much larger Rhine. The wildlife of the tidal river is varied and fascinating and as there are no roads close to this stretch, the cruise is a perfect hide for naturalists. We have seen seal, heron, cormorant and red breasted merganser being carried on the tidal push whilst on the mud of the banks, there is always a variety of waders including oyster catcher, dunlin, curlew and redshank. During the cruise a commentary is given from the bridge pointing out the beautiful riverside villages, salmon fishermen, Greenway House the one-time home of the crime writer Agatha Christie, the boyhood haunts of Walter Raleigh and as Dartmouth is approached the Naval College and the mustering points for the second and third crusades which left Britain for the Holy Land in 1147 and 1268.

Before making this journey, however, there is a little exploring to be done around Totnes, including Berry Pomeroy Castle and the Woodland Leisure Park. Berry Pomeroy, $2^1/_2$ miles from Totnes, takes its name from the Norman family whose coat of arms is carved prominently on the porch of the church. Close by is a medieval tithe barn and the partly 16th century Berry House. About a mile to the north east and sited in a wooded valley are the delightful ruins of Berry Pomeroy Castle now administered by English Heritage. The Pomeroys came over with William the Conqueror but the tower dates to the 14th century. 200 years later it was bought by the Seymour family, the Dukes of Somerset who spared no expense in building spacious living quarters around the courtyard. Below there is a

The Prehistoric settlement near Dittisham.

gaunt dungeon and the place is said to be haunted. Perhaps the ghost is that of Protector Somerset who was executed in 1552 before his house was completely finished. The castle is unusual in the sense that it is a double ruin having medieval walls and an Elizabethan centre. The castle is open daily from April 1st to 30th September. The sinister looking ruin stands on a limestone crag festooned with ivy and undergrowth overlooking Gatcombe Brook another ideal haunt for naturalists.

A visit to the Woodland Leisure Park is a must for those with young families and among its 60 acres (24 hectares) are a toddlers' play village, a commando course, boats for hire on a small lake, an animal farm, nature trails and a picnic field. Here also is the Meadowsweet Honey Farm with 1,000 square feet of indoor exhibitions. This is of interest to all age groups as the life of the honey bee is one of nature's most fascinating stories. The park is open every day from 9.30 am to 7 pm and is situated near to and signed from Blackawton which is on the B3207 between Totnes and Dartmouth. An hotel in the village is now called the Normandy. In 1944 this was one of the Devon villages which was evacuated by its residents to make room for the American troops in training for the invasion of France.

Just upstream from Totnes is Dartington which was built in the 14th century by John Holand whose mother was Joan Plantaganet otherwise known as the Fair Maid of Kent and her influence persuaded the Black Prince to act as his Godfather. It is the largest medieval house in the West of England and the tilt yard still exists although most of it was converted into an Italian type garden by Arthur Champernowne who owned the house during the reign of Henry VIII. The family remained in residence until the early 20th century when it was almost ruined and would probably have fallen down had it not been for Leonard and Dorothy Elmhirst who spent a fortune on establishing a co-educational school incorporating their revolutionary ideas on education. Since the school closed in the late 1980s Dartington has developed into an arts centre plus a college of art and music.

The village of Dartington is pretty in its own right, with the best area being the 14th century Cott Inn which is across the road from Shinner's Bridge. The church dates only to 1878 but it looks older than it is, no doubt in an effort to copy the old estate church which it replaced. Of this earlier church the tower is all that remains situated just to the north of the Hall.

Nearby Dartington is the Cider Press Centre which is open daily from Monday to Saturday from 9.30 am to 5.30 pm and at the height of the season it also opens on Sundays. Cider tastings are a feature but it is also a craft centre selling Dartington crystal, pottery, jewelry, plants and herbs plus perfumes. No cider making is now carried out but the presses are on view. Those who wish to learn about cider making first hand should visit Stancombe Farm at Sherford near Kingsbridge.

Following the A381 and then the B3207 from Totnes to Dartmouth, a brown sign near Dittisham indicates a Prehistoric Settlement. This has been discovered in the grounds of Dittisham Fruit Farm and Capton Vineyard. Here you can buy Blackcurrant, Raspberry, Strawberry and Blackberry Liqueur plus potent sloe gin as well as very pleasant wines made from grapes harvested in late September and October. March 1992 saw television crews descending upon the Farm to feature the Plum wine made from Dittisham plums, a variety of the fruit unique to this area. In addition there is a reconstructed Stone Age Roundhouse with explanations of how the people of the period hunted, cooked and dressed. There is a comprehensive display of flint and pebble tools, pottery, glass, and all sorts of finds from a period of 10,000 years of occupation.

Prehistoric flint tools taken from the village site near Dittisham, now occupied by a successful fruit farm.

Dartmouth is a wonderful old town which has survived German bombers and town planners, the latter often a decidedly more dangerous breed. It is situated about a mile from the mouth of the River Dart but actually there are two settlements here, Dartmouth dominating one bank of the river and Kingswear commanding the other. The railway terminus is at Kingswear and it is linked to Dartmouth by a car ferry. What is now Dartmouth was originally three settlements with Townstall dominating the high land over the harbour. This was probably the earliest of the three as it did not make sense to settle too close to the riverside for fear of invasions. The other two were Clifton which lay to the south and Hardness which lay to the north of an inlet running into the west of the main channel and which was then known as the Mill Pool but which was filled in during the 17th century. By the 13th century, however, development had linked the three areas which together were called Dartmouth. The anchorage was used by the Romans and in the Saxon times a chapel had been erected and dedicated to St. Petrox who died in AD 594. By the 12th century the port was so well established that the second and third crusades sailed from Dartmouth and enterprises on such a large scale must have demanded a substantial back-up of victualling services. 146 ships left for the second crusade in 1147 and 37 for the third crusade in 1268. The import trade was also developing and large quantities of wine was coming in from Spain and especially Bordeau. Being exported was wool and cloth. Edward III granted the town's first charter in 1341.

Dartmouth, unlike many holiday areas, does not close down for the winter and its amenities remain open all the year. The Dartmouth Museum occupies the ground floor of the colonnaded Butterwalk, an attractive 17th century merchant's house conveniently close to the quay. It is therefore not surprising that the museum has a heavily biased maritime flavour. Here are models, paintings and a huge collection of photographs relating not only to Dartmouth, but also to the River Dart. Inside there is a pole staircase which winds close to what looks like a ship's mast, probably because it made sense to a maritime merchant to use the carpentry skills of his men trained in ship-building. The structure also has a 'trip-stair', a device very useful in the days when houses were not lit and flashlights were also devices of the future. Night time intruders would have had to grope about in the dark. The steps were made of varying depths and widths and thus it was very difficult to avoid tripping up and alerting the household. The rooms have also been well preserved and restored following bomb damage in 1943 and there are beautifully pannelled walls and artistically moulded plaster ceilings beneath which it is said that Charles II was royally entertained. Here we found that in 1346 Dartmouth sent 31 ships to help in the siege of Calais and also contributed eleven ships to the Armada fleet in 1588. At one time the port was dominant in the Newfoundland fishing trade. By 1900, however, most of its industries had gone and pleasure boats were its source of income which is still mainly the case. There was a great revival during the Second World War when nearly 500 American vessels gathered in preparation for the Normandy invasions. In those dark and almost disastrous days Dartmouth turned its attention to ship building and around 230 vessels were commissioned including corvettes, minesweepers and air-sea rescue launches.

Dartmouth harbour showing the old railway station which never actually saw a train.

Dartmouth also played its part in the Industrial Revolution even though the town was never scarred by it. The museum has a section devoted to the work of Thomas Newcomen (1663–1729) a local ironmonger who invented the atmospheric beam engine which was later adapted by and made a fortune for Boulton and Watt. An atmospheric engine was erected in Royal Avenue Gardens in 1963 to celebrate the three hundredth anniversary of his birth and this was built in the 1720s and is thought to be the oldest of its type in existence. It first worked at Griff colliery and the last years of its working life between 1821 and 1913 were spent at the Hawksbury junction of the Coventry Canal.

The Henley Museum arose not because of an inventor but because of a private collector proving that the hoarder of today, may be looked upon as the cultural saviour of tomorrow. William Henley (1860–1919) was, like Newcomen, an ironmonger and during his life he educated himself in all branches of art and science and his home on Anzac Street still has his huge collection of organised clutter now looked after by the local council. He wrote funny poems about his job in which he used or sold:-

The United States troops prepare to embark for the Normandy Invasions in June 1944.

'Little drops of oil;
Little bits of wick;
Pennyworth of nails;
Tin of scouring brick.'

On display are William's collection of books, shells, photographs, fossils, his microscope and slides and there is also a reconstruction of his living room.

There are two splendid old dwellings which date to the 14th century which are the Cherub in Higher Street built in 1380 for a wool merchant, and Agincourt House on Lower Ferry also built for a merchant in the same period. An appreciation of the old port can be gained by standing on the cobbled quay of Bayards Cove which has changed little since the sailing ships tied up here and those who remember the classic television series *The Onedin Line* will know it well because it was used as the main set. This was the quay also known to the Pilgrim Fathers. They actually only set out from Plymouth by accident. Originally they sailed in two ships from Harwich stopping off at Southampton but bad weather caused the brethren to put in to Dartmouth and the vessel *Speedwell* seemed to be in worse condition than the *Mayflower*. They set out from Dartmouth on August 20th 1620 and had reached a point 300 miles off

Lands End when it became quite apparent that the *Speedwell* was incapable of reaching the New World and they returned to Plymouth. The *Mayflower* then went on alone and achieved an American landfall at Cape Cod on 21st November 1620. We once crossed to Dartmouth on the ferry on a gentle spring evening and walked from the land point the short distance to Bayards Cove listening to the bells of the parish church blending with the lapping water against the walls of the quay. Here was a true breath of Old England.

Parts of Dartmouth of the 1990s would still be recognisable to the Pilgrim Fathers including the castle, the Parish church of St. Saviour and the artillery forts. Some of the narrow winding streets with overhanging upper storeys of the half-timbered houses, leading up for the harbour would also be familiar. Following a series of destructive French raids in the 14th century it was obvious that Dartmouth had to have a castle. The merchant and mayor John Hawley influenced the building of a fort in 1388 but only the curtain wall and ruined lower fort of this remain. The main castle was begun in 1481 and was the first in Britain to be designed for artillery commanding a harbour as opposed to merely resisting a siege. In addition, at times of danger, a huge metal chain was slung across the harbour from Kingswear Castle, which is not open to the public, on one side to Dartmouth Castle on the other. There is a solid square tower linked to an attached round tower and flanked by a number of gun platforms. In the context of the age this must have been a formidable defence. The main basement was cut into solid rock which gave almost complete protection to the guns whilst the two upper floors were used as living accommodation. In these there is now an exhibition of the history of the coastal defences. The castle is maintained by English Heritage and in summer it opens daily from 10 am to 6 pm and in winter from Tuesday to Sunday between 10 am and 4 pm. Naturally the castle was a focus of interest during the civil war and after a one month siege at the beginning, it was held by Royalists throughout the conflict only being surrendered when all hope for the King was lost and Cromwell's forces were the obvious victors. Improvements were made in the 18th century and again in the 1860s with the Victorians providing accommodation for the crew of five huge guns. Two guns were mounted on the roof

Bayards Quay Dartmouth was used as one of the sets for the classic TV series 'The Onedin Line'.

and one of these is still in position. In 1940 Dartmouth still had a strategic role and the fort was equipped with two 4.7 inch (118 mm) guns. On top was constructed a crenellated brick lookout which to be kind to it is best described as functional. Building projects have never been easy around the castle as the site is limited in size and the old church of St. Petrox is close behind the fortification. Another brick Victorian edifice is a crenellated tower which was once used as a lighthouse.

St. Petrox began as a chapel in 1192 and it is the oldest church in the area but was rebuilt in 1641 in the Gothic style. It is not, however, the parish church. This is St. Saviour's dedicated in 1372 and which owes much of its glory to John Hauley who instigated the building of the first fort and who died in 1408. He is buried in the church after a busy life during which he was Mayor of Dartmouth no less than 14 times! He was a licensed privateer very active in harrying the French during the Hundred Years War and was one of the Commanders of the English Western Fleet. Geoffrey Chaucer, better known these days as a major English poet, earned his living as a customs' inspector and was sent to Dartmouth in 1373 with instructions to persuade the local sailors to reduce their privateering and he must have met John Hauley at this time. It is highly likely that Hauley, who was also one of the town's two Members of Parliament at this period, was used by Chaucer as the basis of the character of an English Seaman in *Canterbury Tales*.

> He rode upon a hackneye, as he coude.
> In goune woolen falling to the knee
> A dagger hangyng on a lace had he,
> About his nekke under his arm adoune
> The hot summer had made his hew all broun;

A more certain epitaph to John Hauley is a fine brass in St. Saviour's church showing a proud and obviously influential man flanked by his two wives. The church also has a magnificent 14th century ironwork door showing prancing leopards in the branches of a huge tree. There is a 15th century screen and painted stone pulpit, with other notable brasses to add to the Hauley monument, an altar dated 1588 showing carved and coloured evangelists and finally an impressive 17th century gallery.

Quite a lot of Dartmouth is built on land reclaimed from the sea and until 1567 the tide actually lapped against the north wall of the church and the attractive houses which now stand on Higher Street also once overlooked the estuary. Close to Bayards Cove are some delightful 17th century houses and also the remains of one of the many castles built by Henry VIII along the coast of England to defend his Kingdom against the French. Just as his daughter Elizabeth feared the Spanish so Henry had to keep a wary eye open for Gallic invaders. Bearscombe castle was built in 1537, and its masonry and gunports guarantee of strength, but there was such a restricted line of fire from its ramparts that its defensive capabilities were almost nil. It is just as well that the Spanish war ship *Nuesta Senora del Rosario* was brought in as a prize ship after the defeat of the Armada in 1588 and had not sailed into the Dart in anger. She remained at anchor in the Dart for a year with the crew used as slaves at Humphrey Gilbert's House at Greenway which was the home of Agatha Christie for more than 30 years up to her death in 1976.

Humphrey Gilbert was one of many 16th century sailors who made a healthy profit by fishing around Newfoundland which he claimed on behalf of England in 1583. He searched hard to find a North West Passage from North America to the East Indies. He was a great navigator in his own right but history has relegated him to being merely the half-brother of Sir Walter Raleigh and both men knew the River Dart very well. The wonderful harbour can be appreciated during the June carnival and especially during the colourful regatta held in late August.

If the regatta is one reminder of a mighty past then an even more historic reminder is the Britannia Royal Naval College for the education of naval officers. The college was first established at Dartmouth aboard a wooden ship called *HMS Britannia* moored in the harbour in 1863. In 1903 a purpose built college was built to the design of Sir Aston Webb who also designed the Victoria and Albert Museum in London. Dominating a hillside site the college was opened by Edward VII and cadets entering at the age of 16 are not only trained in the skills essential to those who will command a ship, but are also given a university education.

Even on a quiet day the harbour is alive with naval vessels visiting the college, fishing boats, pleasure boats and a number of ferries across to Kingswear. This is an attractive place at the head of the estuary, now a sheltered harbour for pleasure yachts and the market centre for the area. Whereas the Dartmouth side of the river was an American base, a house in Kingswear was the focus for the activities of the Free French army. The French still appreciate their old home and in late 1980s President Mitterand made his pilgrimage to Kingswear. The little town clings to a slope and on the flatter land is situated the nearest rail link to Dartmouth, which has now been preserved as a steam railway running to Paignton. Close to the quay at Dartmouth is the old Great Western Railway terminus for the ferry across to the station which is now a restaurant. This is the only railway station which never actually saw a locomotive. It looks at its best when viewed across the inner harbour. The Lower Ferry, which transports cars to and from Kingswear is a quaint and attractive way to travel, but a trip on the steam train should never be missed, and this can also be made from Paignton. The line is 7 miles (11.2 km) long and was first cut in 1864 as part of the Great Western System and when British Rail

The ferry between Dartmouth and Kingswear. The railway station is shown to the right.

closed the line in 1972 it was taken over by the Dart Valley Light Railway Company. Once the first railway reached Kingswear it stimulated the growth of a port specialising in bunkering. New quays and a jetty were built and served ships from all over the world which put into the Dart estuary for fuel, or to collect cargos of stone.

Usually regarded as the capital of South Hams, Kingsbridge rests on a spur of land overlooking a ria which is a drowned valley leading to the sea some five miles away. The layout of the pretty little town consists of a main street with passageways branching off it which is a typical Anglo-Saxon design. It was built on a steeply sloping hill for defensive reasons but historians are not certain why it was given the name of King's Bridge although it did span a small river at the head of a tidal estuary. In the 10th century there may have been several little streams which flowed between the two Royal estates of Alvington and Chillington. These have either silted up or have been built over but can cause minor flooding. The settlement was small and relatively unimportant until 1219 when the monks of Buckfast Abbey provided a commercial focus although the original Saxon lay-out of the settlement was maintained. From the 14th century until the 19th it was a port shipping out wool and metal tools fashioned in local foundries. Later shipbuilding began and there was a regular steamer service to Plymouth. Income was also generated from textiles and flour mills plus the brewing of cider and beer. All these have gone but the tourist industry is booming in the area and one does not need to search too hard to see why. The quiet stretch of deep water is the haunt of attractive yachts and pleasure cruisers often surrounded by swans begging for food but they certainly earn their keep by providing wonderful reflections often framed by graceful trees. Herons frequent the area and have a breeding colony at nearby Holwell which has been established for centuries.

Inexperienced boaters often fail to appreciate the significance of posts sticking out of the watercourse. These mark the channel and if the tide is out boaters can be left stranded for six hours. We know because we did it! Perhaps we would have been better riding along the 1/2 mile track of the miniature railway running along the quayside.

Although it has to be admitted that the area around the car park is far from attractive there are some beautiful aspects to the town and recent housing estates have failed to disturb the original Saxon layout. One way to explore is to follow the Town Crier who makes his tour on most days throughout the year and in truth he has much to shout about. Walking up Fore Street is something of a strain on the breath but those who do not wish to struggle will find yet another car park on the top of the hill close to the Shambles. This was originally built in 1585, extends over the pavement and is supported on a number of stone pillars. There has been a rebuilding but the name tells that the area was used as butchers' shops and slaughter houses during the 18th century – it would have been a shambles in every sense of the word. Close by is the Town Hall built in 1875 and topped by an onion shaped clock tower which we have seen described as a 'slate hung ball clock'. Whatever it is it is beautiful. It is also unusual in having only three faces as one of the sides faced the old workhouse and it was considered that the inmates did not need to know the time!

Two other buildings in the town which should be visited are the parish church of St. Edmund and the Cookworthy museum both of which are situated on Fore Street. The spire of the church can best be seen from the street in front of the clock tower. St. Edmund's was established in the 13th century prior to which the people of Kingsbridge had to travel to Churchstow two miles to the north west and situated on a steep hill. The older people must have been particularly grateful to have their own church. St. Edmund's is, or rather was, a rich man's church with no room for unattached women or the poor and this led to Roger Phillips making a social comment on his gravestone following his death in 1798.

> 'Here lie I at the chancel door,
> Here lie I because I'm poor,
> The further in the more you pay
> Here lie I as warm as they'.

Roger whose nickname was Bone lived as he died, as the local eccentric scratching a living collecting plants for apothecaries and hiring out his services as a whipping boy. This practice was widespread whereby those with money could pay those less fortunate to take their punishment. Most of the church itself is 15th century and there are some good carvings and elegant monuments but it has been altered considerably since then, but our lasting memory is always one of Roger Phillips.

The Cookworthy museum on Fore Street is open from Easter to the end of September from 10 am to 5 pm Monday to Saturday and during October from 10.30 am to 4 pm. There are lots of rural life museums springing up these days but the Cookworthy is livelier than most having collections of costume, farming implements and carts plus a Kingsbridge estuary exhibition. It is named after a local man, William Cookworthy, the son of a Quaker weaver born in 1705. His father died when William was only 13 and leaving his mother to bring up her family of five. Undaunted, William walked to London, managed to get himself apprenticed to a chemist and apart from learning his trade the young man taught himself Greek, Latin and French. By 1726 he had become sufficiently well thought of to be made a partner in a wholesale chemistry firm but in 1745 history almost repeated itself with the death of his wife leaving William with five daughters. His luck turned when, after many years of trial and error in the true scientific spirit resulted in his discovery of kaolinite, a combination of feldspar and Cornish clay from which he produced the first 'hard paste' porcelain which became much sought after as it took colours easily. William got some inspiration from sailors based at Plymouth who brought porcelain back from China and all it took was a chemist with the knowledge to realise that Cornish 'china' clay was the ideal material in which to copy the orientals. There is a collection at Plymouth and another in the Cookworthy museum. As naturalists we found the pictures of wild flowers, mammals and birds to be both attractive and accurate. The building which houses the museum is of interest in its own right being the one time Grammar school founded in 1670 by Thomas Crispen. He was born in Kingsbridge but made his fortune in Exeter from his fulling business. Still on view is the headmaster's canopied seat elevated on a platform above which are the arms of Charles II. Oak pannelling covers the walls covered by initials carved by generations of scholars. Now we call these interesting but in those days the scratchings were just graffiti.

At nearby Woodleigh the Woodland Trust have saved a stretch of the valley of 'the little River Avon'. Included are the botanically rich woods of Bedlime, Titcombe and Woodleigh itself. Running alongside is a section of the disused railway line between South Brent and Kingsbridge.

Stancombe Farm is the place to discover Devon Cyder and is reached off the A379 road to Dartmouth. Most cyder production is carried out in November yet another reason for exploring the South Hams region out of the tourist season. The press used is a twin screw machine more than 200 years old situated in a thatched building overlooking the orchard of 500 apple trees. The apples are crushed and placed in an envelope in a wooden frame. This is the only variant from the old method which used straw. The press is operated by hand and the juice pours along a channel into a tank from which the barrels are fitted. Apples contain natural sugar, enzymes, tannin and yeast. Within four days fermentation has started, is completed in four months and is then ready for drinking.

Stancombe is set in a rural South Hams valley about $3\frac{1}{2}$ miles out of Kingsbridge and the manor was mentioned in the Domesday book. In 1582 the Manor was gifted to Sir Francis Drake by Queen Elizabeth as a reward for his round the world trip. Although there is a lot of holiday accommodation these days the old character of the hamlet remains and visitors are

Slapton Ley looks at its best after rain.

made very welcome at the cyder farm. The taste of the traditional English amber nectar is wonderful.

Not only is Kingsbridge an ideal base from which to explore the rich heartland of the South Hams, but is also close to one of Britain's most beautiful coastlines.

Once again it was our interest in natural history which attracted us to the area and we came to study the area around Slapton Ley and Sands where so many informative courses are run by the Field Studies Council who have here a Residential Centre. During the summer season the staff also run day courses and guided walks for the benefit of visitors. The area is best viewed from the road between Dartmouth and Kingsbridge. The Ley is an area of freshwater measuring almost 2 miles (3.2 km) long by a maximum of 1/4 mile (0.4 km) wide separated from the sea by a high ridge of shingle and flint, materials which as we have seen, have caused navigational problems on many rivers in South and East Devon. The maximum depth seldom exceeds 10 feet (3.6 metres) and this makes the Ley an ideal place to support rich colonies of emergent plants and a most unlikely site for the last resting place of King Arthur's sword Excalibur. Slapton Ley is but one of the suggested resting places for the magical weapon with others spread across the length and breadth of England. At one time it seems that there were two lagoons but the northern expanse is now largely overgrown with reeds, but the southern ley still has open water and provides sport for trout fishermen, good hunting for botanists and exciting spotting for ornithologists. It was the birds which first attracted us to Slapton on a February morning with a clear blue sky and a gentle but icy-fingered breeze. We identified many species of wildfowl including wigeon, tufted duck, pochard, scaup, shoveler, mallard and red breasted merganser. There is a ringing station here run by the Devon Bird Watching and Preservation Society. Bird ringing is not an occupation for eccentric amateurs but a highly professional, solidly scientific and internationally co-ordinated enterprise. Marking birds has a long history and Romans were known to net adult swallows on their nests and taken away to the chariot races. A coloured thread was tied to the bird's leg indicating the identity of the winner of the race. When released the bird flew straight back to its nest where eager punters were waiting to place a bet! Early attempts were made to mark valuable birds of prey belonging to rich individuals and a peregrine belonging to the French King Henry IV (1589–1610) carried a gold ring on its leg. It was lost from the chateau of Fontainbleau and was recovered a day later on the island of Malta having flown a distance of 1,350 miles (2160 km). It took a long time for the scientific world to accept this ringing technique which in America is known as banding. In 1902 a scientist called Bartsh began to ring birds using bands each with a unique serial number and an address, to which the ring could be returned should the bird be found dead or examined closely enough to allow the number to be read. Information from ringing can reveal how long birds live, how far and in which direction they travel. Small birds are caught by spreading a delicate mesh looking almost like a badminton net and this is the main method used by the workers at Slapton Ley who catch large numbers of warblers, swallows and martins which roost among the reeds mainly during their autumnal migrations.

Slapton village is also worth an extended visit and has a history, both ancient and modern. Sheltered in a gentle fold of the South Hams the soil is so fertile and the air so warm that crops are grown with a speed which would do credit to many tropical areas and there are still signs of the Saxon method of strip farming in the surrounding fields. Although the church has been clumsily restored much of interest remains including the impressive 14th century spire, a sanctuary ring in the porch which the pursued could grasp and claim protection providing he or she confessed and then left the country by the shortest possible route. As the coast was so near this can hardly have presented a problem. Inside the church are tombs of the family of John Hawkins the Elizabethan sailor who was not averse to adding to his income by indulging in a spot of piracy or slave-trading. He used some of his ill-gotten gains on embellishing his manor house at Poole just to the north of Slapton. Even more impressive than Slapton church itself is the 80 foot (24 metre) tower, all that remains of a chantry college founded in 1373 by Sir Guy de Brien, Lord of Slapton Manor and the Steward to King Edward III. Slapton's more recent history is revealed by two artefacts – a monument and a tank. In 1944 thousands of American troops trained here and in many other parts of South Devon in preparation for the D-Day landings. The local people were moved away from their homes during this period. It is no surprise to find a monument to record this event but the Sherman tank overlooking the southern edge Slapton Ley close to Torcross is an unusual sight on a nature reserve to be sure. The tank was dragged out of the sea in 1984 and has now been restored as a memory to nearly a thousand Americans who died on exercise in the bay when they were surprised by German E boats. This stretch of the South Devon coast including Slapton

An American Sherman tank on the Slapton Dunes.

can be discovered by using Salcombe as a base and examining Start Bay, Beesands, Hallsands and Start Point all of which are delightful places. After a day exploring Salcombe, Bolt Head and Bigbury Bay can be enjoyed at leisure.

There is an exciting approach to Beesands via narrow lanes down to a single row of ancient dwellings once the home of lobster, crab and mullet fishermen who hauled their boats almost up to their cottage doors. Fishing trips can still be arranged with the boatmen and some of the old atmosphere of the hamlet remains despite the presence of motor boats which are for hire and a caravan site to the north.

Hallsands from a historical point of view has not fared as well as Beesands as the fishermens' cottages are now mostly in a ruinous condition and on a shelf of rock at the foot of a cliff but not repaired following a devastating storm of 1917. This disaster could have been prevented if tons of protective shingle had not been removed in 1897 to provide building material for extensions being made to the docks at Davenport. There is no doubt that Hallsands has atmosphere and it deserves its share of visitors. The battered old cottages reminded us of the Hebridean island of St Kilda left by the local population in the 1930s and now the haunt of birds.

Disasters were once common events hereabouts and on one stormy night in 1891 five ships were smashed to pieces on

In the 1920s Beesands was a busy lobster fishing village. This photograph shows Shingle Street. It is situated between Dartmouth and Start Point.

the rocks below Start Point. There is a good car park on the headland from which a short stroll leads up to the lighthouse and from which there are obviously wonderful views over Start Bay, the word Steort being Anglo-Saxon for a tail. This also accounts for the name of the redstart a lovely bird of the thrush family and which has a red tail. The resort dominating the area is Salcombe with its harbour protected by the headlands of Prawle Point and Bolt Head. Prawle is an Old English word meaning a lookout, which was its precise function. There is a car park near the village of East Prawle and from this a pleasant footpath connects with the long distance South-West Coastal footpath and then via a row of coastguard cottages to Prawle the most southerly point in Devon and from which there are wonderful views. Geologists visit this area to study formations known as raised beaches. These were caused when sea levels were higher than at present and the sea eroded the rocks and the new beaches were infilled by shingle. Over thousands of years raised beaches were produced and Start Point is an ideal place to study a series of these. It is possible to follow a footpath

Salcombe Harbour.

from the Point into Salcombe via East Portlemouth and a foot ferry. In summer Salcombe can be crowded, but in the off-peak periods it is a most attractive place.

The river which feeds the old port is technically a Ria which is defined as a drowned river valley. Because it is so sheltered the harbour known to the Saxons is still the haven of boatmen and hundreds of yachts snuggle into the 2000 acres (80 hectares) of tidal creeks. The quay is still lined with boatyards and chandlers' shops and there are many reminders of the days when merchant ships sailed in from the West Indies and the Mediterranean bringing spirits and spices which made the merchants rich. In the mid-18th century the mild climate attracted the wealthy who built villas and established yet another of Devon's fashionable resorts. Although its port still functions Salcombe depends upon tourism for its livelihood. Its history, including its role as an American mustering point for the D-Day invasion of Normandy, is told in the Town museum housed in the old Customs' House on the quayside. Close by at Sharpitor is another museum, now owned by the National Trust. This is open from 12 noon to 5 pm between Easter and the end of October. Overbecks Museum has a fine collection of Victorian photographs, the story of the maritime history

Salcombe photographed in the 1930's.

of the area, as well as a display of natural history. This can serve as a stimulus to proceed beyond the house and walk the footpaths around Bolt Head. Refreshments are served at the museum and there is a thoughtfully arranged secret room for children, and the gardens are truly memorable. The National Trust also maintain these footpaths which are well marked and from them we watched stonechat, circling seabirds and sat quietly in sheltered dells full of the scent and colour of coastal flowers. Lantern Rock was once just that – a rock on which a lantern was perched before lighthouses were built. From the site of yet another Devonian Iron Age Fort there are views of Bigbury Bay and across the Plymouth Sound to the city where our journey of discovery ends.

CHAPTER 6

East Devon

If South Hams can boast to be the most fertile area in Devon it must surely be seriously rivalled by East Devon. Here along the River Axe is produced a high proportion of the Devonshire cream we all love. Here also lived some of the great Englishmen. Walter Raleigh was born near East Budleigh, Winston Churchill's ancestor the first Duke of Marlborough near Axminster and Samuel Taylor Coleridge, author of the *Ancient Mariner*, at Ottery St Mary. Part of the income of the area came from wool which tended to be concentrated on Tiverton and Cullompton between the 15th and 18th centuries. Tiverton is on the border between North and East Devon, and which we described in our companion volume *Discovering Exmoor and North Devon*, but Cullompton is an ideal centre from which to explore the eastern area as are Axminster, Honiton, Axmouth and Seaton, Branscombe, Sidmouth and Ottery St Mary. In the next chapter we will follow the coast from Dawlish to Brixham.

Cullompton's church tower rises 120 feet (36.5 metres) above the small market town and was partly financed in 1526 by John Lane a wealthy wool stapler but there were substantial contributions from other wool merchants. They set out to rival Tiverton's church which was also financed by merchants particularly John Greenway. Cullompton has a delicately coloured and beautifully crafted wagon roof which was regilded in 1859, a vast and quite remarkable screen, a Jacobean gallery with impressive carvings and an additional aisle with a fan vaulted stone roof which must have cost John Lane a tidy sum of money as he tried to keep up with the Greenways. This is a church which should not be rushed but time must be taken to examine the carvings, many of which have a combined religious and business themes. Here are angels holding sheep shears and teasels which were used to raise the nap on the cloth. Prior to a devastating fire in 1839 Cullompton must have been graced by some wonderful buildings but some of the Victorian replacements do not jar on the eye and must have helped to produce a pleasant coaching town and linked well into the older buildings which survived the fire. The Manor House Hotel for example, retains its 1603 features although it was enlarged during the 18th century and close by is Walron's, a private house built between 1603 and 1605 for a wealthy lawyer named John Peyers. It is made of rubble stone in a central section of three storeys with two storey wings flanking this and provided with rows of neat mullioned windows.

Just to the north east of Cullompton is Kentisbeare, dominated by St. Mary's church which has an even more impressive screen than Cullompton's and dates to the 15th century. Buried in the churchyard is E. M. Delafield who spent the last 20 years of her life at Croyle on the highlands close by. Her most famous work was the *Diary of a Provincial Lady*. The screen was the work of craftsmen from Tavistock Abbey and whilst working they were probably accommodated in Priesthall, a medieval church house near the graveyard. This wonderful building has an oak screen of its own and a fine minstrels' gallery.

Axminster is synonymous with the word carpet only rivalled in England by Wilton but as we shall see, the two are intimately connected. There was, however, life before carpets in this attractive little market town. In the late 7th century there was a West Saxon settlement here and there was probably people living here at the time of the Romans as modern Axminster lies at the intersection of two vital Roman roads – the Fosse Way and Ichnield Street. Archaeologists suggest that the site may have been settled prior to Roman times and the Roman roads may have been but an improvement on the ancient green tracks of the Celts. It is the Saxon settlement, however, of which there is hard evidence. Here it was that Athelston, the son of Alfred the Great, established a College of Priests and it was this minster on the banks of the River Axe which accounts for the present name of the town. The Normans also recognised the strategic position of Axminster and it was they who began the splendid church and the arch over the south-east door is obviously original although there have been many additions since the 12th century with a major reconstruction during the early 13th century, much of it funded by Alicia de Mohon who died in 1257. The tower is her lasting memorial although she also has a commemoration to her life inside the church.

Each Thursday there is a market which has been held since the Charter was granted by King John in 1210. This would have been an outlet for the woollen and agricultural produce of the Cistercian abbey situated at the confluence of the Axe with the River Yarter. This must have been a mighty abbey and experts have managed to work out from the very few remaining bits of masonry that the church measured 280 feet (85 metres). Such a building required money and it was the Cistercians who established Axminster as a major centre for the production and processing of wool. This continued long after the abbey had been dissolved around 1538 but it was only in 1755 that a local weaver Thomas Whitty began to produce the carpets which made the town famous. Whilst looking around the markets of London's Cheapside he saw a huge Turkish carpet measuring 36 feet by 24 feet (10.9 metres × 7.3 metres) and determined to work out how such a wonderful piece could have been woven without any seams. It is a tribute to his skill and his determination that on Midsummer's Day 1755 he produced the first Axminster and began a history which still continues but which has not been continuous. The carpets were slow and expensive to produce and it is said that when each one was completed a message was sent to the church whose bells were rung in celebration, and the finished carpet carried to the church in a procession. Anyone wishing to see Axminster at its best should visit the church which is carpeted giving a warm soft feel to the venerable old building. Although this is a modern addition the church does have on display a genuine Thomas Whitty original. Such was the reputation of Axminster that the Sultan of Turkey paid £1000 for a carpet around 1800. The business prospered until 1835, but at that time the management seemed to go awry on its costings and the company went bankrupt. The looms were sold to a factory at Wilton, a company now just as famous as Axminster. The final demise may have been partially brought about in 1827 when Whitty's factory on Silver Street burned down but Thomas's house which stood close by survived and the two storey building is now the Law chamber. In 1937 a new factory was opened and Axminster carpet was produced once more and visitors are welcome by appointment to view the process of weaving. The factory is situated on Woodmead Road which is close to the railway station which itself is worth close and admiring attention. It is Gothick in style and built for the South Western Railway in 1859 to connect Salisbury and Exeter. Prior to the coming of the railway, Axminster was an important stop on the coach road which is now on the line of the A35 between Dorchester and Honiton. Apart from the church the other building dominating the town centre is the George, a magnificent example of an old coaching inn. At Dalwood, near Axminster, is Burrow Farm Gardens which since 1967 has covered a five acre site created from an ancient Roman clay pit. The Gardens open daily from April 1st to 30th September between 2 pm and 7 pm. On Sundays, Wednesdays and Bank Holidays homemade cream teas are served. There is ample parking and a good picnic site. From the gardens there are wonderful views and the woodland gardens have a happy balance between wild and garden flowers. The plant nursery is very popular especially at weekends.

What Axminster is to carpets so Honiton is to lace. Apart from its own obvious attractions Honiton is an excellent centre from which to discover East Devon. Accommodation is good and varied to suit each taste and budget. From the Blackdown Hills to the north, to the coastline in the south the majority of the countryside is designated as an area of outstanding beauty and is within easy reach of Dartmoor, Exmoor and Exeter. It has always been one of the important gateways into Devon and has been known to motorists for many years although the centre has now been sensibly bypassed. It is also on the rail route between London and Exeter. Standing on the banks of the River Otter which rises on the Blackdown Hills in Somerset and flows to the sea at Budleigh Salterton, Honiton is a residential market town with a population of around 8,000. It made its early living from cloth manufacture and later, because of its lace, substantial buildings were constructed but there were a series of disastrous fires in the 18th century which destroyed many gems. Some of the replacement buildings, however, are very elegant.

The town has a long and distinguished history, but world famous because of its lace. The story of the town is told in the

Although Honiton is regarded as the lace capital of Devon many other places claim the title. This dress is on display at Otterton Mill.

Allhallow's Museum which is run as an independent registered charity and staffed by volunteers. It may be run by amateurs, but it looks professional and for a small fee it can be visited from the end of April to the end of October from 10 am to 4 pm (5 pm in the season). The museum, situated next to St Paul's church in the town centre, does not open during the winter or on Sundays. The displays are housed in part of the former Allhallow's chapel which was built in the 13th century and a former school dining room dating from the 18th century. The so called Norman gallery is the place to discover the story of Honiton lace, which has been made in the town since about 1560 and once the tradition was established the trade spread over East Devon and West Dorset, but Honiton, although challenged, never lost its supremacy. It soon achieved world fame and whilst searching the craft shops of Malta where lace making is not only an art, but almost a religion, we found specimens of Honiton lace displayed with pride. By the year 1698 more than half the population of the town were engaged in lace making and men, women and children all played their part in meeting an almost insatiable demand. Like many other crafts hand lace-making declined during the 19th and 20th centuries as cheap machine-made products cornered the market. Many local people still make lace as a hobby, and craft shops often have pieces for sale. These make unique presents to remind the discoverer of the joys of Devon. In summer the museum organises demonstrations of the craft and there are occasional demonstrations in September and October as and when volunteers are available. In the Nicol gallery the history of Honiton from prehistoric times to the present is chronologically displayed. The bones of hippos found in the area have been dated to the time 100,000 years ago when Devon was just as tropical as Africa is today. The bones came to light during the construction of the bypass! Life around Honiton in the Stone, Bronze and Iron Ages is depicted not by the usual method of glass cases full of neatly labelled artefacts but by using imaginative models showing what the people and their dwellings may have looked like, plus some of the actual tools found in the area. The Murch gallery is concerned with more recent industries including pottery which has a more continuous record in Honiton than lace making as it continues commercially right up to the present time. The work of Charles Collard is well represented. Another fascinating feature is a coin operated machine explaining and demonstrating the Devonian accent most useful for 'foreigners' like us, and it is also essential that such features of a county should be preserved. Finally in this excellent museum it is possible to buy postcards, books, and materials relating to lace making and it provides what we always love to discover – items which are unique to the area being visited.

Two areas within a car journey of Honiton which deserve a long visit are the Farway Countryside Park and Hemyock Castle.

Situated five miles to the south of Honiton, Farway Countryside Park and Nature Reserve is signposted from off the A375 road to Sidmouth close to the Hare and Hounds Inn. There is an entry fee to the 100 acres of grassy plateau from which there are woods running down to the Colne valley and the views are always good whilst on a clear day they can be breathtaking. In 1990 the complex changed hands and the theme altered with more emphasis on the preservation of the native wildlife and pesticides banished from the area. The Butterfly House for which a small extra payment is required, features the conservation of British species but there are also exotic species in the tropical conservatory. There is a resident herd of red deer plus 'retired' ponies and donkeys and an assortment of farm animals including pigs, sheep, poultry and a flock of white doves. There is an on-going scheme of planting native trees and a leaflet explains the Nature Trail and the wild creatures to be found along it. There is a cafe which is also licenced, a gift shop, a childrens' play area and dogs are welcome if kept on a lead.

Hemyock Castle is the ancient stronghold of the Hidon and Dynham families situated five miles south of Wellington and which is open on Sundays and Bank Holidays from Easter to September and on Tuesdays and Thursdays in July and August. In all cases the opening time is from 2 pm to 5 pm although schools and other groups are welcome at other times by prior appointment. There is a car park and a picnic area but no refreshments are available on site although the nearby Catherine Wheel public house has tasty bar snacks on offer. The Castle Interpretation Centre illustrates the life of the castle from medieval times until the 20th century with artists' impressions and full size tableaux. It is also possible to visit the dungeon. The Hidons were allowed to crenellate their manor house which was already fortified in 1380 and four turrets and the curtain wall are still standing. The moat still contains water much to the gratification of mallard and moorhen.

Some of the history of this pretty village, which in 1886 developed the first butter factory in the West Country, is displayed on the walls of the Catherine Wheel. Here is told the story of the Popham family who were the patrons of the attractive 13th century parish church of St. Mary. Although some of its early atmosphere remains the interior suffered badly

Typical Devonian cliff scenery seen here at Seaton.

when in 1768 the arches of the nave were clumsily ripped out taking with it much of the quality of the interior. An unusual feature to be seen, however, is in addition to the usual list of rectors the sextons are also listed. Their duties included whipping any unruly dogs out of the church. These days we must wonder why dogs got into church in the first place, but in medieval times people often travelled for many miles over dangerous country and they brought their dogs with them as protection. They also made use of nearby Inns for stabling their horses and for their own much needed refreshment.

One of our favourite ways of exploring the coastline of East Devon and its borders with Dorset is to follow the A358 from Axminster to Axmouth and then using the B roads to Seaton, Beer, Branscombe, Salcombe Regis, where we spent our honeymoon more than 30 years ago, and into Sidmouth. All this takes in the beautiful sweep of Lyme Bay where the Devon Axe feeds into the sea.

To the Romans the Axe estuary was a crucial port and before it silted up the largest of their ships could safely navigate up to the sheltered harbour at Axmouth. This is overlooked by Hawkesdown Hill, the site of an Iron Age fort, which according to legend is haunted by a formidable warrior and his fire-breathing dog. From the Roman port the Foss Way, one of the most important roads into Britain, began its journey. In the church are the substantial remains of the Roman presence plus some well preserved medieval wall paintings and the tomb of Roger Hariel an influential vicar who died in 1324. Excavations have proved that Axmouth was a large Roman settlement but silting by gravel and pebbles over the centuries have meant fewer human activities but this has proved to be of great advantage to the wildlife. The B3172 follows the estuary from Axmouth to Seaton and although the road can be busy there is parking on the riverside of the road. There is a tramway running along the same route and for those who want easy views then a journey on the top deck of a tram is recommended, especially during the holiday season. The tramway runs for three miles and takes in Colyford and Colyton where there is a gift shop and childrens' adventure playground at the terminus. Light refreshments are available all day at the station tea rooms. There is plenty of parking here and also at the Seaton terminus.

Like all estuaries, however, the Axe is at its best between late September and April when, depending upon the state of the tide, the variety of bird life can to say the least, be exciting. Here we always see cormorant, curlew, redshank, mute swan, mallard, oyster catcher, dunlin, wigeon, teal and lapwing whilst on more notable days we have watched kingfisher, goldeneye, bar tailed godwit, greenshank, dabchick, red breasted merganser and ruff. Just a mile to the south of Axmouth are splendid sea cliffs which are always under threat from erosion with the worst recorded incident being in 1839 when an estimated 6 million tons of earth crashed down. This has since been first stabilised and then colonised to produce a varied habitat now protected as a Nature Reserve.

Seaton also has a history dating back at least to Roman times and there was also a medieval settlement on the seafront, but by the 16th century this had been strangled by a bar of stones which defeated all efforts of the local people to divert their river around it. The initial exports were wool brought from the Cotswolds and lead from the Mendips. By the time of Domesday eleven salt works were in production. By the 17th

Fishermen's boats at Beer land fresh fish each day which is on sale in a nearby cabin.

century they accepted the inevitable and built a bank to allow the land behind it to dry out and create some pasture. In the 19th century a branch railway was built along the banks and it was this which was converted into the tramway between Seaton and Colyton which we have already mentioned. The Axe is now crossed by a substantial arched bridge made of concrete designed by Phillip Brannon and when it opened in 1877 was one of the first of its type ever to be built.

Seaton continued to earn something of a living from fishing but local landowners slowly began to tune in to the mid 19th century Victorian's demand for sea breezes and healthy holidays. The town is still tuned into this need. The climate of most of the East Devon resorts is good being protected by Dartmoor from the damp south westerly winds. Seaton is a pleasant blend of Edwardian and Victorian development, although some of the church of St. Gregory survived a fierce restoration of 1868 and the late 13th century window is a joy. There are no other monuments or historic buildings but this is made up for by colourful and aromatic gardens, and a beach backed by tall cliffs of chalk on one side and red sandstone on the other. There is a good Information Centre and a rather attractive little museum.

Beer, despite its name, is renowned for its beautiful scenery, and especially its stone which has been quarried since Roman times. Beer stone has been popular for so long because it is easy to cut and once exposed to the air it quickly develops a hard outer coat. Exeter cathedral and many of London's buildings made great use of Beer stone. Part of the quarry, about a mile west of the village, is now open to the public and there is an exhibition of the tools used by the old quarry men. The quarry is open between Easter and October from 10 am to 6 pm and it is possible to join a guided underground tour to see some of the old workings dating back to Roman times. Those who want to see Beer stone used in vernacular architecture should stroll around the village itself which is a colourful mixture of stone, thatch and clean paint. A pleasant little stream runs down a culvert to the sea and adds its own music to one of Devon's most attractive villages. We love walking down to the tiny sheltered harbour, its walls hanging with wallflowers and to sit among the fishing boats and lobster pots. Here is a fresh fish shop, where we stock up our freezer with dover and lemon sole, cod, haddock and mackerel.

Beer, perhaps with some justification, challenges Honiton's claim to be the centre of the Devon lace industry. The locals assert that survivors from the Spanish Armada and then Flemish refugees from religious persecution brought lace making to Beer. Their product was later taken to London by stage coach via Honiton and this town then usurped the title of the Lace Capital. In 1839 a thousand poundsworth of lace made in Beer was used to trim Queen Victoria's wedding dress. Our love for Beer stems from its lack of hard commercialism, with its simple fishing, especially for crabs, and there is no better feeling than to enjoy a thick crab sandwich on the verandah of one of the pretty beach hut cafes. The beach is safe and so clean that it never has any problem in satisfying the EEC regulations. In the season it is possible to hire a motor boat and look back at the coastline which soon shows why Beer was once the haunt of smugglers. The most notorious was Jack Rattenbury, born in 1778 and who was so elusive that the customs' officers could not pin him down and he earned the name of 'Rob Roy of the West'. There is a display devoted to him in the museum at Budleigh Salterton. A visit in August, to coincide with the village regatta, is to be recommended and the people of Beer prove to be adaptable and hospitable as extrovert visitors are allowed to join in events on water or on dry land whilst those of a more withdrawn nature are allowed to watch from a distance. There is plenty for children to do and one of their favourite treats is a ride on the miniature railway at Pecorama Leisure Park which runs through colourful gardens, with the added attraction of a clean safe beach.

Within a gentle drive of Beer on the Sidmouth road, is a Country Park near to which is the well signed Iron Age settlement of Blackbury Camp, freely open and maintained by English Heritage. The hill fort was protected by a bank and ditch in the shape of a D and a triangular extension called a barbican was begun but never completed. It was inhabited by a cattle farming community for around 100 years beginning 200 BC. These days it is a quiet sheltered spot for a picnic and echoes with bird song in spring including chiff-chaff, blue tit, willow warbler and pheasant.

Before proceeding down the coast to the equally attractive village of Branscombe some time should be given to the discovery of Colyton and Colyford. Colyton has a history dating back at least to Saxon times and a cross standing in the churchyard of St. Andrew's has been dated to AD 900. The present church is actually on the site of a Saxon Minster and much of it is 14th century, especially the very unusual octagonal lantern tower. Some damage was done by a fire in 1933, but remaining on the north side of the chancel is the damaged effigy of Margaret the Countess of Devon, the granddaughter of John of Gaunt and who died in 1449. There is also a monument to Sir John Pole who was a dominant 17th century worthy, and his wife Elizabeth. Other buildings of interest are the vicarage built in 1529 and the 17th century church house which functioned as the local grammar school until 1928. A look at the shape of the modern village still reveals its Saxon origins, arranged in a circle with the streets running off this to provide the maximum protection from invaders. Although there are plenty of inns and tea shops if the weather is good the local food shops should be discovered, a picnic gathered together and enjoyed at the site at the edge of the village from which there are wonderful views over the Axe valley. This is walkers' country and there is the Foxglove Way Footpath which runs through Colyton to Budleigh Salterton. Only established in 1990, this is already very popular but there are always places along it to satisfy those who wish to be alone with wildlife.

Colyton holds a regular 'Petticote Lane' market on Saturday and also has its carnival in September. Not to be outdone, nearby Colyford has its 'Goose Fair' in late September and it is then possible to see the games and crafts known to the medieval residents including tossing the straw bale. The local folk enter into the spirit of events by dressing in traditional costume. The church at Colyford was only a chapel-of-ease to Colyton and has a relief modelled on Bartollomeo's famous masterpiece called 'The Entombment'.

Branscombe is situated about four miles to the west of Seaton and although it is open to the sea it is protected by surrounding hills. The winding lanes lined with lovely cottages do not create a natural centre, but it is safe to assume that life revolved around the fine old Norman church dedicated to St. Winifred which is famous for its medieval wall painting of Belshazzar's Feast and an 18th century three decker pulpit. A look at the base of the tower reveals the herringbone work typical of the Saxons. Within the church is a priest's dwelling, a feature which was once common in the days when the shepherd never strayed far from his flock. There is also a very strange monument to Joan Tregarthen who died in 1583 but outlived two husbands and bore twenty children! Her tomb is in the shape of a Greek temple.

As at Beer the villagers of Branscombe were once skilled in lacemaking, and they also claim to have contributed to Queen Victoria's wedding dress. Alas the lacers have gone, but the stream in which they washed their finished pieces is still there and unpolluted. There is some debate regarding the origins of its name. One suggestion is that its position at the foot of a branching comb or valley accounts for the name whilst some historians believe that Saint Branwalader or perhaps Branwellanus was buried here as early as the 4th century. The village is mentioned by name in the will of no less a personage than King Alfred and in AD 925 there was a church here governed by the Benedictines from St. Peter's at Exeter. The manor is mentioned in Domesday as was the Church Living a building opposite the church and which was replaced by the present structure in the 16th century. Its original function was probably to house the monks from Exeter whilst conducting their business affairs in and around the village.

We love this village with its thatched cottages and a couple of quaint hotels. There is a pottery here and the old blacksmith's forge still shoes horses, the thatched bakery produces deliciously smelling bread in ovens traditionally heated by twigs of ash. Once more we have a village at the focus of wonderful walking country, now recognised as such being part of the increasingly popular East Devon Heritage Coast.

Surmounting a wooded hill to the west of the Fountain Head Hotel is a prehistoric site consisting of barrows and earthworks. From the village there is a choice of a road or a wood-lined footpath leading to the car park by the shore, where thatched tea rooms provide a pleasant spot to rest. To the left of the rooms is the so-called Castle Rock and a number of chalk pinnacles created as a result of a huge landslip during which more than ten acres shuttered down towards the sea. This has now mellowed beneath a fragrant carpet of vegetation and a walk along the coastal path leads to an unrivalled view of Lyme Bay.

Any honeymoon is memorable, but some are more memorable than others and ours at Dunscombe Manor at Salcombe Regis falls firmly into the second category. It was all because of the bees and nothing at all to do with birds! On the morning of the last day of our fortnight, with a long drive in front of us a huge swarm of bees settled all over our caravan their bodies sealing all windows and the door and we only escaped five hours later when their keeper, advised on their whereabouts by the site owner, came dressed in his uniform and armed with a smoke gun to remove them. Despite this we have returned time and time again to stroll round the byways of Salcombe Regis with its attractive thatched cottages and which has changed hardly at all over the years.

The Regis part of the name derives from the Kings Alfred and Athelstan who were the owners of the manor which had its rich salt pans on lease to the monks of Exeter. Salt deposits were even more vital in the days before refrigeration as meat and fish had to be salted in order to keep it fit to eat. Wherever there was an area of shallow sea, efforts were made to evaporate the brine and the resultant salt was jealously guarded. The Roman soldiers had part of their wages paid in salt and this was described as their salarium from which our word salary derives. Many manors, including Royal Salcombe, were valuable assets because of the tax paid on their salt deposits. Apart from a rather fine 15th century eagle lectern there is little within the 12th century St. Mary and St. Peter's church to commend it but on the outside are a couple of fascinating things to see, both concerning 'other worlds' but in startling contrast. In the lych gate there is what looks like a huge bolt but is actually a tool used by body snatchers and known in that trade as a 'resurrection corkscrew' and which was designed to prize open coffins. In the days when medical students found difficulty in obtaining bodies on which to practice their skills, they were reduced to stealing recently dead bodies and paid body-snatchers to keep up a supply of corpses. The 'corkscrew' was abandoned as late as 1880 when two Sidmouth doctors and their muscle man were disturbed and obliged to flee. A much more pleasant route to Heaven was searched for by the astronomer Norman Lockyer who is buried in the churchyard. Lockyer also discovered Helium and keeping him company in the hereafter is Sir Ambrose Fleming, the inventor of the radio valve. How strange to find two brilliant scientists buried in the churchyard of such a tiny village. It does, however, show that they had an extra genius at work when they chose where to end their days. Just to the south west is Salcombe Hill on which stands an observatory founded in 1912 by Lockyer and which is now part of Exeter University's astro-physics programme.

During the 19th century Sidmouth became one of Britain's most fashionable seaside resorts and the best remaining example of the style of Regency architecture known as cottage orné. It is typified by many unusually shaped windows, balconies of wrought iron, or wood carved to look like wrought iron, with polished door knobs and with the prominent colour being either white or cream. This type of architecture is seen at its best along and close to the mile-long Esplanade and the adjacent York terrace. These contrast with the white cliffs of Beer Head and also with the red sandstone cliffs which rise to heights of 500 feet (152 metres). When she was only seven months old Princess Victoria was brought to Sidmouth for her first view of the sea, but by then it was already well established as a resort. The future Queen's family did not visit the area because of its obvious beauty, however, but to escape from creditors. Her father was then the Duke of Kent and the family stayed at Woolbrook Cottage which is now known as the Royal. In 1820 the Duke died and although Victoria never returned to Sidmouth she did present the parish church with a stained glass window in memory of her father. Sidmouth was given great stimulation during the wars with Napoleonic France during which the rich, deprived of the French resorts, turned instead to their own country as far away from the French-facing coast as possible.

For those who wish to discover the history of the resort then a visit to the Sidmouth Museum is essential. There are old photographs, paintings and prints, samples of lace, a costume gallery and a few irrelevant but fascinating items such as a tobacco pouch made from the foot of an albatros and a bloody-looking sign advertising the skills of a barber surgeon. Parts of old Sidmouth have been lost including the old parish church demolished and given a spartan replacement in 1860. Some of the old church was removed to construct the old chapel situated just off Heydons Lane and is a fascinating jig-saw of a place. Those interested in sporting history should not fail to visit one of England's most attractive cricket grounds which dates to 1820. It is a lovely place to sit and picnic especially on a summer Saturday whilst listening to the sound of willow striking leather. For those who wish to sit quietly without watching sport then the Duke of Connaught's Gardens are ideal and were presented by a grateful visitor in 1934 in gratitude for four quiet winters spent in the resort.

Although usually genteel Sidmouth does leap into life during early August when it hosts a musical festival which deserves to be considered as a serious rival to the Eistedfodd at Llangollen in North Wales. Dancers and musicians from all over the world flood into the west country and add their colourful costumes and rich heritage to that of one of Europe's most beautiful resorts. The vibrant happy noise of the festival contrasts sharply with the scenery around Ladram Bay where motor boats and canoes can be hired and where pleasure and fishing boats have been a feature for more than a century. The coastal scenery is spectacular and the sound of lapping waves is often gentle and soothing.

Before continuing along the coast of Devon's Riviera there is one more inland town which should be discovered and few

Ladram Bay was beautiful and popular with tourists from Sidmouth when this photograph was taken almost 70 years ago.

settlements are more beautiful than Ottery St Mary. We were once travelling on the London Underground between Euston and Kings Cross when we picked up a printed piece of A4 paper bearing the title 'A *Guide to Ottery St Mary*'. This was all we could understand because the rest of the text was written in Japanese! The date was the 4th November and on the following day we were journeying into Devon and seeing a sign for Ottery St. Mary we decided to pay a brief visit only to find ourselves in the middle of the Tar Barrel Ceremony now part of the Bonfire Night celebrations. The ceremony was performed long before Guy Fawkes and the Gunpowder Plot. It may well have originated as a sun worshipping ceremony and an effort to persuade the relevant gods to return the sun in time for the following summer. The ceremony involves keeping traffic from the streets whilst burning barrels of tar are rolled down a hill but kept in check by men with their arms protected by thick sacking. In Victorian times strenuous efforts were made to ban the event which had become so unruly that police reinforcements had to be drafted in from Exeter.

Ottery St Mary is, however, a town for all seasons with a fascinating history. Here was the birthplace of Samuel Taylor Coleridge of *Ancient Mariner* fame and the town also has one of the finest churches in Devon. Apart from its 'organised' fires Ottery St Mary had had more than its fair share of disastrous infernoes during the 18th and 19th centuries which destroyed most of the medieval buildings. It is still, however, a fascinating little town snuggled on the East Bank of the River Otter and its narrow twisting streets leading up from the river are a joy. The Georgian houses in any other town might be the centre of attention but here everything is dominated by the church of St Mary which has played such a rôle in the life of the town that it has become part of its name. In its early days St Mary's was nothing more than an average parish church, but its destiny was then fashioned by Bishop John de Grandisson who gave instructions for the production of a smaller edition of his cathedral at Exeter. His scheme was largely accomplished by 1342, a remarkable feat when we consider that a college for priests at Ottery was only instigated on 22nd January 1337. What a wonderful job was done for there are so many exciting things to see in the Collegiate church which flourished for over

The lovely old church at Ottery St. Mary.

The clock at Ottery St. Mary is based on a similar pattern to the one in Exeter Cathedral (see p. 14).

two centuries. Kings Henry VI and VII were entertained at St. Mary's but this did not influence Henry VIII who dissolved the college in 1545, although the church was allowed to continue as the parish church, and many of the furnishings remain and are in fine condition. Included is a 14th century astronomical clock showing the moon and the planets and which still has its original workings, a carved and brightly coloured altar screen, medieval oak stalls, bench ends and a gilten eagle lectern in the Lady chapel. The vaulted ceilings are also richly coloured as are the corbels and bosses. There are the canopied tombs of Sir Otto de Grandisson who died in 1359 and his wife Lady Beatrix who passed away in 1374. Postcard and guide books are on sale within the church.

Before its dissolution the college had buildings set on three sides of the churchyard, but these were mostly demolished. The Choristers' House and the Choir School occupied the south side. Following the Dissolution, Henry VIII insisted that the school should be renamed the 'Kynge's Newe Grammar Scole of Seynt Marie Ottery' which has since been replaced by the King's School on the western fringe of the town. Samuel Taylor Coleridge was born on October 21 1772, the thirteenth and youngest child of the Rev. John Coleridge who had two wives and was the vicar of Ottery St Mary and the Master of the King's school. Sadly this building was demolished in 1884 and the site is now part of the garden of Grandisson Court. A bronze plaque on the wall is all there is to remind us of the poet who died in 1834. When you stand back in the gardens and look up you can see what is said to be the oldest weathercock in the country and has an ingenious system of tubes through which the wind whistles.

Crossing the Otter is a 16th century bridge and from here an avenue of lime trees leads up to Cadhay. Alas this historic house is not open as often as we would like but it is well worth while making careful plans and paying the entry fee to explore it. It opens on Spring Bank holiday and then on Tuesday, Wednesday and Thursday in July and August plus the late Bank Holiday. Apart from this group visits can be arranged by prior appointment at reduced fees. Cadhay is mentioned during the reign of Edward I (1272–1307) when it was listed as a Sub-Manor of Ottery St Mary and owned by the de Cadehay family. The main part of the present house was built about 1550 by John Haydon who had come into possession of the house when he married the Cadehay heiress. The rebuilding, however, was carried out in a very sensitive manner by retaining the Great hall of an earlier house including the fine timber roof dating to 1420. John's successor added a splendid Elizabethan Long Gallery overlooking a magnificent courtyard. Alterations in the 18th century added a Georgian

Budleigh Salterton in the 1950's.

aspect to this fine building, the history of which is explained by the well informed owners.

Cadhay is attractive at any time, but on a hot summer's day it is at its best with pollen dripping from the lime trees and bees buzzing heavily among the pale green leaves.

Before leaving East Devon there is one region left to explore which is the coastal strip from Budleigh Salterton.

Few people may know Budleigh Salterton, but most have seen the sea wall of the resort as this forms part of Sir John Millais' painting of *The Boyhood of Raleigh*, which was exhibited at the Royal Academy in 1870. There is a plaque on the wall of Octagon House to indicate that the artist stayed in the area whilst working on the painting. He used his two sons and a local ferryman as his models. There is no doubt that Raleigh would have known this coastline as he was born just inland at East Budleigh and in the church is a pew which bears the coat of arms of his family. At this time the River Otter was navigable right up to the village, but as we have seen there has been a great deal of silting up in this area.

Sir Walter Ralegh (1554–1618), as his name is sometimes written, was born about 1554 at Hayes Barton almost two miles from East Budleigh and which is also signed from the latter along a footpath. The house is not open to the public

Budleigh Salterton April 1992.

and is a thatched farmhouse built about 1450 but at least this historic place is in good repair. Some would love it to become a museum devoted to the life of one of England's finest men who lived a life of high risk and great adventure. All Devon lads had seawater in their blood and Ralegh had good connections as Sir Humphrey Gilbert of Greenway House between Totnes and Dartmouth, mentioned in chapter 5, was not only one of England's most respected sailors but also Walter's elder half-brother. The young man was sent up to Oriel College at Oxford, but despite a very active brain he was not suited to the cloistered life of a student and after less than a year he headed for France where he fought with the Huguenot forces and was present at the battle of Montcontour in 1569. He spent a period in London doing what can best be described as odd jobs in and around the Inner Temple after which he found his first true niche as an explorer and coloniser. He established his reputation first in Ireland and rose to command the siege of Smerwick in which more than 600 Spanish mercenaries were killed which impressed the poet Spenser and delighted the 'Faerie' Queen Elizabeth herself. Whether he actually laid his cloak over a muddy pool or not he became a Royal favourite, but blotted his copy book by secretly marrying the virgin Queen's handmaiden Bess Throckmorton in 1592. In 1595 Sir Walter decided to try to restore his position in an abortive mission to find gold in Guiana, which is now known as Venezuela. This was quite a voyage in those days, but nothing to the Devon sailors. Although this scheme failed, Ralegh's leadership of an expedition to sink Spanish shipping in Cadiz Harbour in June 1596 delighted Elizabeth. By careful

A millwright at work at Otterton Mill in the 1870s.

diplomacy Walter avoided being implicated in the problems of the Earl of Essex and had the Queen lived longer all would have been well. In 1603 she died and when James Ist came to the throne he listened to Ralegh's enemies who accused him of high treason and Walter and his family were imprisoned in the tower for thirteen years from 1603. Had he not had this time on his hands Walter Ralegh might have been too busy to earn a reputation as a writer although he had already published some poetry and very readable accounts of his travels. *The History of the World*, published in 1614, was the masterpiece of its age and covers Greek, Egyptian and Biblical History up to 168 BC. Eventually he was released on the promise that he would return to Guiana and bring back gold. This failed again and was a disaster for him as his assistant Keymis committed suicide and his eldest son was killed. On his return to England the King bowed down to Spanish pressure for revenge, Ralegh was rearrested on the old charge of treason and 29 October 1618 he bravely mounted the scaffold and was beheaded.

Brighton, Southend and Blackpool are seaside resorts used by generations of music hall comedians to depict the common

A Devon water mill around 1880.

man at play, whereas Budleigh Salterton was lampooned as the resort of the 'posh'. The pink shingle and pebble beach stretches for two miles from Otterton Lodge to Straight Point and shelves deeply so that only good swimmers should wade into the sea. It was the shingle as opposed to sand on the beach which prevented too much exploitation, and the area is also overlooked by high crumbling cliffs known as the Floors. There are pleasant and gentle walks beside the River Otter where ships were once loaded up with salt and wool before

Otterton Mill now a delightful craft centre, but still grinding some grain.

the waterway finally silted up in the 15th century. The story of the village is told in the little museum which since 1967 has occupied Fairlynch House and which is open during the summer and at other times by appointment. The thatched building was constructed in 1811 and around 1838 it was the home of the eccentric Rev. W. S. Heineker who was just as much a scientist as a cleric. He invented a lathe designed to make screws and some of his drawings and blueprints are on display. There is also a smuggling exhibition with specific reference to Jack Rottenbury from Branscombe. Before leaving the Budleigh Salterton – East Budleigh area, Bicton Park and Otterton Mill should be visited, especially those with young families to entertain. Bicton, reached through the village of Colaton Raleigh, has a fine avenue of monkey puzzle trees and the obelisk dominating the south of the park close to the lake are both famous, the latter being a focus for the surrounding district. Apart from this the once elegant gardens laid out in the mid 18th century for Lord Henry Rolle and influenced by André de Notre, who created Louis XIV's garden at Versailles, are now almost, but not quite swamped beneath the tangle of

Although quite rare the Painted Lady can be found on the warm days of early autumn close to Otterton Park near Budleigh Salterton.

a commercial Theme Park. It is still possible to find sheltered spots including a summer house with its floor paved by the bones of Bicton park deer, shrubs and trees brought back by the Rolle family from Florida and the Bahamas and a remarkable little shell house made from specimens brought back from the beaches of Exuma island in Bermuda. We once found an urgent young man walking around this house and making constant and careful reference to a world book of shells! Also to be found is the family mausoleum built in 1850 to a design by Pugin and standing in the ruins of an old and no doubt interesting parish church now sadly replaced by the modern and unimpressive church of St. Mary situated to the south east. There is one gem to be found in St. Mary's and this is a fine memorial to Dennis Rolle who died in 1638 and was moved from the earlier church. It was carved by Nicholas Stone of Woodford who later became famous and carved the memorial of John Donne in St. Paul's Cathedral in London. Bicton Park is open from 10 am to 6 pm between March and October.

Otterton Mill can be visited by car, but for those with the time and inclination to discover on foot there is a delightful walk from Budleigh Salterton. Leaving the Lime Kiln car park at the end of Marine Parade the walk is well marked and follows stretches of the bank of the River Otter frequented by grey wagtail. There are also good views of the estuary and the rookery in Otterton Park. This is also butterfly country and on a hot August afternoon we identified red admiral, green veined white, meadow brown, grayling, common blue and peacock. Sometimes in late summer or early autumn the migrant Painted Lady is seen but dies at the onset of cold weather. On a springtime walk on a damp May morning we identified yellow iris, bluebell, knitbone, lady's smock and the glorious golden yellow blooms of marsh marigold. Otterton Mill was restored in 1977 and it is known that corn has been ground on the site since before the Norman Conquest. It is open throughout the year from Easter to the end of October between 10.30 am and 5.30 pm and from 1st November to Easter between 11.20 am and 4.30 pm. There is a bakery and the Duckery Restaurant. Wholemeal bread is baked and organic flours are on sale in the shop as well as cakes, scones and pastries. In the winter the Duckery is often closed and then snacks are available from the bakery but during the season the Duckery is open daily and its cream teas are something rather special.

The mill itself is a lesson in social history and there are two wheels each 10 feet (9.3 metres) in diameter which were made by the Bodley brothers of Exeter in the early 19th century following the design of a French engineer named Poncelet the inventor of the breast-shot wheel. The mill machinery which drives the wheels is also of interest and is part wood, part cast iron and dating from the 18th and 19th centuries. The great spur and crown wheels have cogs made of applewood. Milling is usually carried out on three days each week, but the machinery is operated each day for the benefit of visitors. In the mill museums there are illustrations of the working of the mill. On the stone floor there is a relief map of the River Otter pointing out the position of the corn mills which long ago operated along its length. There are also displays of stone-dressing tools and all the stages of fashioning the wooden machinery is explained. A tape recording is played once each hour and explains how the mill was restored, and there is also a display of its history. The miller himself often takes groups around his beloved domain. Upstairs among the twisted timbers is a display of Devon lace. As we try to discover the various counties, each has thrown up special places – Otterton Mill is one of these.

Exmouth has always been one of our favourite winter resorts because of our lifelong interest in natural history. Those who do not know the area should first visit the Tourist Information Centre on Alexandra Terrace which has details of guided nature walks which are organised throughout the year. In winter the estuary of the Exe is alive with thousands of wildfowl and waders including Brent geese and the avocet, the long legged black and white wader with the upcurved bill made famous as the symbol of the Royal Society for the Protection of Birds. Birdwatching cruises are also organised from Exmouth harbour and there are also a number of pleasant walks along the shoreline. Exmouth is close to Woodbury Common a spectacularly colourful area dominated by gorse and heather with pleasant stands of Scots Pine. Apart from the interest of the fauna and flora there are wonderful views of the estuary.

Exmouth developed early as a seaside resort because it was so close to Exeter and a reasonably good road connected the two. Then came the railway and for some reason Brunel's route did not feed Exmouth but followed the west side of the Exe estuary and thus allowed the development of rival resorts at Dawlish, Teignmouth and Torquay. It was 1861 before a branch line reached Exmouth by which time it was too late to catch up with the tourist trade. Although Exmouth can still be regarded as a dormitory settlement for Exeter there remain reminders of its former glory and the splendid beach is underated by many guide books. The advantages the resort had are still obvious. The beautiful coastal scenery, especially the western area, were particularly attractive to visitors in the late 18th century who were, as we have seen, deprived of their visits to France. Prior to this time the only visitors to the Exe were Algerian and Tunisian pirates during the 16th and 17th centuries and in 1688 the Dutch also sailed no fewer than 140 vessels up the river to Topsham. By 1765 peace was guaranteed and Exmouth was described as 'the Bath of the West, the resort of the tip-top of the gentry of the Kingdom.' Development for tourists was initially dovetailed into the ancient fishing village although silting prevented larger ships from penetrating too far up river. Some fishing is still carried on, and a channel is kept open to the port. During the early 1800s tourism and ship building were carried on side by side. A line of elegant Georgian houses was built and attracted the wives of Lord Nelson, the sailor, who earned his title and Lord Byron the poet who inherited his. Such influential visitors acted as a magnet for others anxious to join the famous. At this time the port was still thriving but Exmouth owes much to the Rolle family who we have already met at Bicton, and several local monuments are named after them. It was Lord Rolle who started to build the promenade which was later extended towards Orcombe Point to produce a delightful Marine Drive. This leads to Orcombe Rocks owned by the National Trust and a wonderful spot to enjoy a scramble and search for interesting coastal plants including harebell, eyebright, rest harrow and bird's foot trefoil, the latter often called bacon and eggs because of its blend of red, yellow and orange colours. In the middle of the Esplanade is the Victorian Diamond Jubilee Clock Tower surrounded by a mass of colourful flowers growing in the shelter of the gardens, an area enjoyed by those of more advanced years. In contrast the children are well catered for in discreetly sited amusement areas behind the beach.

   Those who enjoy the unusual and have a feel for English eccentrics should not miss seeing an interesting house known as A-La-Ronde, built in 1795 just to the north of the town centre. It is unique buildings such as this which distinguishes one resort from another. Miss Jane Parminter and her younger cousin Mary modelled their house on the plan of the circular church of San Vitale in Ravenna. From their fifteen acres there are magnificent views over the Exe and here the ladies lived as true feminists allowing no mere male anywhere near them and well away from their plans. Only unmarried female members of the family were allowed to inherit but this has been relaxed

A-La-Ronde, built in 1795, and one of the most unusual houses in Britain.

and the Parminter connection is still maintained and they are much more tolerant of visitors than their ancestors would have dreamed of being. After the death of her cousin, however, Mary Parminter spent more than 30 years developing a chapel surrounded by a group of almshouses which she called 'Point in View'. The original almshouses have been replaced by larger and more comfortable dwellings but five unmarried ladies are still accommodated close to Mary Parminter's chapel which can be visited on foot from 'A La Ronde'.

Exmouth has retained its docks dominated by towering cranes, the smell of diesel and full of quaint ale houses and more up market pubs and restaurants. The food on offer here is plentiful, delicious and the price is reasonable. Much fun can be had watching large cargo vessels being skillfully manoeuvered into the dock basin via a narrow channel which looks very like a canal even though it was never constructed as such. Apart from in the docks area, Exmouth has a number of historic pubs including the Ship on the High Street, dating from around 1700, and the Deer Leap which began life as a bathing house at the time that the resort was establishing its genteel reputation.

Exmouth Museum and the Library are both on Exeter Road and we have used both to discover the history of the area, particularly on one day in January when snow swept across the area, almost closed the roads but totally blocked out the scenery. Exmouth has plenty of accommodation on offer ranging from high class hotels to self-catering or caravans of all shapes and sizes. For those self-catering we especially recommend an early morning trip to the harbour where it is possible to buy fresh fish and shellfish direct from the boats.

Before leaving Exmouth the passenger ferry which operates in summer, should be taken across to Starcross and for those with children the World of Country Life at Sandy Bay is a memorable day out. At Starcross is the recently restored atmospheric pumping station designed by Brunel. It is the great inventor's only failure. The idea was based on the supposition that locomotives would not have the necessary strength to pull their rolling stock up the steep incline between Newton Abbot and Exeter then run by the South Devon Railway. It worked on a very simple idea of creating a vacuum within a continuous pipe laid between the track and into which ran a piston which could be connected to the leading vehicle of the train. Pumping houses were arranged at intervals along the track and which sucked air from the pipe thus producing a vacuum, and the passing train was dragged into the vacuum section as its piston allowed air to rush into the empty pipe. The idea sounds so simple that it is hard to see why it failed, but among the excuses put forward was that rats were chewing through the leather seals. Whatever the reasons, and there were probably many, the project was abandoned in 1848 having lost around half a million pounds which was an enormous sum in those days. The brave enterprise is commemorated in the preservation of one of the 'atmospheric towers' as a working museum. Brave visitors can be whizzed up an inclined track with the system powered by a Heath Robinson-like contraption using vacuum cleaners!

Sandy Bay's Country Life Centre is open from Easter until October from 10 am to 5 pm. On display are more than 100 farm implements covering around 150 years of agricultural history and there are slow motion demonstrations of the techniques of milling, threshing and other harvesting methods. There is a collection of horse drawn vehicles and early tractors. We enjoyed the reconstructed gamekeeper's cottage, typical of the 19th century which is filled with the tools of his trade plus simple furniture and ornaments of the period. There are collections of steam engines, vintage cars, bicycles, fire engines and the machines once used to drive fairground rides. Here too are 'Victorian' shops with modern sections with goods on sale plus a craft studio, adventure playground, picnic site, gift shop and a restaurant. Once the entry fee has been paid there is a 'free' Safari train journey passing red, Sika and fallow deer, white highland cattle, soay sheep and llamas. Children are encouraged to stroke rabbits, lambs, wallabies, goats, donkeys and ponies. Sandy Bay cannot be properly explored in less than half a day, but those with dogs should make alternative arrangements especially if the day is very hot and they cannot be left in the car.

For those who would not enjoy a longish walk from the passenger ferry from Exmouth, then it is best to cross the bridge at Exeter and follow the A38 signed Plymouth whilst looking out for signs leading left to Starcross and Sandy Bay. Continuing along the A38 on to Dawlish heralds the start of the English Riviera.

CHAPTER 7

The English Riviera

Although it is the resorts of Torquay, Paignton and Brixham which jointly claim the title of the English Riviera, the whole of the coastline from Exmouth to Plymouth is a relatively unpolluted stretch of glorious scenery. A coastal drive with a few gentle diversions will lead to a discovery of Dawlish, Teignmouth, Newton Abbot, Torquay, Paignton and Brixham and so into Plymouth and the Cornish boundary which is described in the final chapter.

> Over the hill and over the Dale
> And over the bourne to Dawlish
> Where Gingerbread wives have a scanty sale
> And gingerbread nuts are smallish.

This is not vintage Keats to be sure but as youngsters reading poetry books this rhyme introduced us to Dawlish long before we ever visited the area. Our first visit was many years ago on a blazing hot July afternoon with the blue sea sparkling in the sunshine and Dawlish Warren Nature Reserve at its colourful best with a large number of its more than 450 species of flowering plants in full bloom. The Warren can be reached either by road or rail, but our favourite route is on foot although care needs to be taken during high tides especially if a strong breeze is blowing off the sea. Langstone Rock composed, like the rest of the cliffs, of red sandstone, has a tale to tell as steps were cut into it by customs' officers in order to reach the top and keep a look out for smugglers and wreckers. The latter earned a good if heartless living by hanging lights along the coast designed to confuse ship's navigators who thus sailed their vessels onto treacherous rocks. The wreckers then gathered the merchandise from the debris. In the period following the Ice Ages the melt water raised the sea level and waves crashing into rocks fragmented the cliffs and created a huge sand spit now known as Dawlish Warren. The first written record dates from 1280 when it was used as a hunting ground; in the 16th century a defensive fort was built and in 1782 a number of sailors were buried here having fallen in a battle with the Dutch which was fought just off the coast. There were also salt works on the Warren and in the 19th century the area called Greenland Lake yielded oysters with 1867 being a boom year when 28,000 succulent shells were harvested. At this time the Warren consisted of two parallel sand spits with the Greenland Lake trapped between them. The outer spit eroded, the lake drained and it is now the car park. The Warren was used by the RAF during the Second World War and in 1974 an area of 55 acres was designated a Nature Reserve. Guided tours are given by the Warden and details of these can be obtained from the local Tourist Information Centre or from the Warden's own Visitors' Centre.

The history of the area is explained in Dawlish Museum which is open daily between May and September on payment of a small fee. Here is a Victorian kitchen, shop, parlour, nursery and bedroom. The history of the local railway is also explained. To say the least the siting of Brunel's railway, which arrived in 1845, was insensitive. It was constructed in a straight line across the shore and effectively separating the settlement from the sea. This is one of the best and safest places in Britain to take a swim. The railway gives something back to the town as the station has been little altered since its construction and is itself a museum piece. There are convenient car parks around it and beneath the platforms is a busy little cafe.

Although now an attractive seaside resort Dawlish did warrant a mention in the Domesday book and a Saxon village was situated just less than a mile inland, well away from invaders, but only a few thatched cottages now mark the spot. As the settlement expanded towards the sea in the 19th century a small stream was straightened and the valley floor landscaped in order to support first Georgian and then Victorian villas. Wealthy and influential visitors arrived including Jane Austen and Charles Dickens, both very well travelled people considering the age in which they lived. Jane Austen used Dawlish in *Sense and Sensibility* as the honeymoon venue of Lucy and Robert Farrar whilst Dickens set Dawlish as the birthplace of Nicholas Nickleby. The centre piece of modern Dawlish is known as the

Lawn which was once a swamp populated by heron, kingfisher, moorhen and otter. In 1808 John Manning used the earth removed during the construction of Queen Street and Strand Hill to raise the level of the land and despite being almost swept away in 1810 it was restored and is now solidly established. The Lawn is beautifully landscaped and through it run cascades of water with calm areas between providing feeding grounds for the mallards and other birds which delight the children. It is sandwiched between a happy conglomeration of shops, cafes and amusements and whilst we were looking for photographs for this book we met the Town Crier, his voice seeming to bounce off the water and drown the sound of the weirs.

Teignmouth was also a popular Georgian seaside resort and Jane Austen also spent some time here in 1802 and in 1818 John Keats and Tom his sickly brother, rented a house at Northumberland Place. The elegant three storeyed house is known as Keat's House although some have suggested that the brothers may have rented property on the opposite side of the road where the Drake's Head Hotel now stands. By all accounts the weather was not kind but Keats did manage to compose some verse including the frivolous one about Dawlish quoted earlier and on a more serious note he also wrote the introduction to *Endymion*. As the 19th century progressed Teignmouth developed an elegance due to such building complexes as Powderham Terrace, the Den and the two mile long Esplanade along the seafront. A pier was built around 1860 and in its early days this divided the bathing area into two – half for men and half for women. The playground of Teignmouth however was only a veneer over a busy port dominated by its shipping. The tide is swift here and twice each day the channel is given a good scouring and no ship enters the harbour without a Trinity House pilot aboard. From the 16th century Teignmouth has been Dartmoor's port and from its quays granite left on its journey to build many of London's landmarks including London Bridge and the British Museum. Ball clay from the Bovey Basin has also been exported via Teignmouth, and the quayside and Customs' house are still busy at the present time. There is a long distance footpath called the Templar Way from Teignmouth leading into Haytor in the heart of Dartmoor.

Teignmouth initially developed as a port because of the fishing industry including Newfoundland cod and also fish caught in the channel itself. Although the industry has declined there are still fishing vessels sailing out of Teignmouth and their character is in contrast to the colourful but clinical lines of pleasure craft. The best way to appreciate the harbour is to take the little passenger ferry across to the picturesque Georgian village of Shaldon, a service which now runs regularly during the summer, but whose origins date at least to Elizabethan times. There is a village green, used as a bowling green in summer evoking memories of Drake, and surrounded by a cluster of shops which attract tourists like bees to honey. Wednesday is the best day to visit Shaldon because the local people dress up in 18th century costume. A pleasant stroll leads down to Ness Cove via a genuine smugglers' tunnel, the Ness itself being a headland which protects the village and allows Shaldon to remain snug in its own little time warp. For those who enjoy their food and drink in lovely surroundings then here is a choice of restaurants and cream teas which are as fine as any in Devon.

Although most of this chapter is concerned with coastal resorts, time should be allowed for a trip inland to Newton Abbot. Situated at the head of the Teign estuary and straddling the River Lemon one of the small tributaries, Newton Abbot which was given its market charter in 1220 advertises itself as the gateway to Dartmoor and the Coast. It is difficult to argue with either of these boasts. Each Wednesday farmers with their round faces and equally round Devonshire accents converge on the market to buy and sell cattle, sheep, pigs and poultry. An antique market is held on East Street from 9 am each Tuesday, and although the early closing day is officially still Thursday, fewer and fewer shops are complying with it. There is also a busy Saturday market and a butter and pannier market each week day and for those who are discovering the area and in self catering accommodation here is the place to spoil yourself with home-made jam, biscuits, cakes and local cheese and eggs.

The centre of the town is dominated by the tower of St. Leonard's church standing at the junction of four streets, Courtenay, East, Bank and Woolborough. The rest of the building was demolished when a new church was built on

Woolborough Street in 1836. If the stones of the tower could speak they would tell of the day when a little bit of British history was made on the steps of the church and which is commemorated by a plaque. In November 1688 the Dutch husband of Queen Mary stayed at Forde House and was proclaimed William III, Prince of Orange who promised to be 'the glorious defender of the Protestant religion and the liberties of England.' Forde House was built in 1610 and was designed by Sir Richard Reynell to an E-shaped plan which came into fashion in Elizabethan times. The building was dovetailed onto an even earlier manor house.

At the other end of the town is Bradley Manor looked after by the National Trust and situated just off the A381 road to Totnes. The house is surrounded on three sides by steep wooded slopes and set low in the valley of the little River Lemon. A dwelling had been listed at Bradley at least from the 13th century but it is its 15th century wing which demands attention and admiration as one of the West Country's best examples of Gothic architecture. In the south wing, however, there is the undercroft dating to the mid 13th century. In 1909 Cecil Firth the archaeologist sensitively restored the Manor and in 1938 his daughter presented it to the National Trust. The family are still in residence but Bradley Manor is usually open on Wednesday afternoons.

Those wishing to delve deeply into the history of Newton Abbot should visit the Museum in the Town Hall which is open Monday, Tuesday, Wednesday and Saturday from 10 am to 4 pm. Aspects covered include geology, archaeology, houses such as Bradley Manor, Forde House and Sandford Orleigh. There is also a selection of photographs of Brunel's Atmospheric Railway and also of the Great Western Railway when Newton Abbot was the centre of a carriage repair works which employed more than 600 people. There is a small railway museum also in the Town Hall building. It was obviously a railway town but prior to this Newton Abbot was set at the cross roads of the Exeter to Dartmouth Turnpike. The reason for the town developing this way was because of its position at the head of the Teign estuary and the focus of several valleys. On race days Newton Abbot returns to its glorious past as visitors descend upon it by road and rail and most of the major roads leading to it are blocked with horse trailers. We choose race days to have a gentle boat trip from the Town Quay and potter slowly down the river to Teignmouth.

Race days are also likely to result in the local country parks being quieter than usual, although it is always possible to find places to study the wildlife in peace. Bakers Park, Courtenay Park and Stover Park which has a 14 acre (5.6 hectare) lake surrounded by extensive nature trails which are always fascinating. Decoy Park is 100 acres (80 hectares) of rich woodland set around another lake, and punctuated by a network of footpaths. There is also a childrens' paddling pool and playground plus a picnic site and course fishing is available on the lake.

There are three other places which should be visited before leaving the Newton Abbot area – Tuckers Maltings, Twiggie Winkies Farm and the Gorse Blossom Miniature Railway and Woodland Park. For more than a century Tuckers Maltings on Teign Road and quite close to the racecourse, have been roasting barley to produce malt for brewing beer, the man in charge of the process being the Malster, now a fairly common surname in Britain. Audio video programmes and guided tours explain the process,but the lasting impression is the smell of the malt. The maltings are open daily from Easter to the end of October from 10 am to 6 pm with the last tour being at 5 pm. Coach and school parties are welcome and there is a meeting room available with facilities to show videos. John Barleycorn's cafe serves good food and gifts can be purchased from the Magic Malt Shop.

Twiggie Winkies Farm is on Denbury Road about $1\frac{1}{2}$ miles out of Newton Abbot off the A381 road to Totnes. There is an extensive car park big enough for coaches and mini-buses. It is open from 12 noon to 6 pm each day from Easter to the end of September. In 1991 the owners opened a hedgehog hospital and the children love to see the prickly patients being restored to health. Many hedgehogs die because they fail to build up sufficient fat during the summer and one of the functions of the hospital is to fatten up their patients, although they do treat a number of road casualties and collect many which fall down cattle grids and unless removed would starve to death. There is a farm adventure trail and a variety of animals to get close

Babbacombe Beach photographed about 1900.

to including donkeys, hens, ducks and rabbits. Youngsters can help to bottle feed lambs and ride tractors. There is a cafe and farm birthday teas can be laid on when requested. Above all Twiggie Winkies is a friendly farm.

Gorse Blossom Miniature Railway and Woodland Park is near the village of Bickington about 4 miles to the north of Newton Abbot. It opens between Easter and early October, and also around Christmas. The complex is set in 35 acres of oak-dominated woodland of which almost half is open to the public and there are wonderful views of the Teign valley and Dartmoor. The nature trail is well worth following even by those who consider themselves to be serious naturalists. The entry fee to Gorse Blossom includes car parking, admission to the grounds, unlimited rides on the miniature railway and all facilities – there are no further charges except for refreshments and souvenir purchases.

To discover the English Riviera proper, we must continue to Torquay, another ideal place for a winter holiday as the climate is most pleasant and no doubt because of this most of the surrounding attractions remain open throughout the year. Close to the harbour on Babbacombe Road is Torquay Museum and is one of the best of its type which we know. It

Torquay photographed during the First World War. Look at the concentration of warships outside the harbour.

opens Monday to Saturday from 10 am to 4.45 pm and also on Sundays from July to mid-September. It is owned by the Torquay Natural History Society which was founded in 1844. The present museum was opened in 1876 and its collection is vast and only a small fraction of its treasures are on display at any one time. It is always worth chatting with the staff in the museum office about specific queries. The museum should be of interest not only to students of Torquay and Tor Bay but by those interested in Dartmoor and South Devon in general.

In the impressive entrance hall is a model relief map of the area with extended notes carried on panels. There is a mock-up of a Bronze Age Kistvaen or burial chamber typical of those found on Dartmoor and there are also some ancient carvings taken from nearby Waddenton Court. There is a collection of local rocks and fossils, a vast collection of prints and photographs illustrating the development of Torquay as a seaside resort. The Laycock gallery is devoted to a local girl called Agatha Christie, born in 1890, and here are photographs, newspapers, book covers and posters. There is on display the hat, scarf and handbag used in the television series *Miss Marple*.

Torre Abbey, the finest and most historic building in Torquay.

First time visitors to the museum will have their appetite whet for a visit to Kent's Cavern which is described in the Archaeological gallery. The caves are open from 10 am seven days a week throughout the year except Christmas Day and closing at varying times according to the season. From April to June they close at 6 pm, during July and August at 9 pm (except Saturdays when it is still 6 pm). During September and October at 6 pm with winter closing being at 5 pm. There is easy access via only nine steps with a constant temperature of 52°F (11°C) and lit by electricity. The caves are situated just inland from Anstey's Cove and the spacious car park can be reached by following the brown signs. Kent's Caverns are not just a showpiece for the tourist but one of the world's most important archaeological sites. The discovery of human remains here changed the fundamental ideas of the antiquity of man. There were people here during the Stone Age, but long before this the caves were used as shelter by sabre toothed tigers and mammoths. The remains were carefully examined first by Thomas Northmore and John McEnery in the 1820s, but most progress was made by a Cornish Quaker named William Pengelly. He left school at 12 but educated himself during sea voyages aboard his father's vessels. He came to Torquay feeling sufficiently qualified to open his own school in the late 1820s. Once the study of the caves gripped him Pengelley devoted the rest of his life to unravelling their secrets. Despite his contribution, however, the caves are not named after him but after Sir Kenneth Kent, a favourite of Edward II and who had been offered shelter by Sir Henry Lacey who lived near Torre Abbey following the murder of the King at Berkely Castle near the Forest of Dean in 1327.

The Spanish Barn at Torre Abbey.

Legend suggests that Henry Lacy planned to betray Kenneth Kent but he was warned by Serena, Lacey's daughter and she and the fugitive sought refuge in the caves. It is said they never emerged but there has never been any sign of their bodies. Perhaps they were lovers who escaped to live happily ever after or maybe they perished. In any event we wonder why their story has never been woven into a novel particularly in the heart of Agatha Christie Country.

The caves are a joy and so is Torre Abbey which was founded in 1196 by William Brewer in thanks for the deliverance of his sons who had been held hostage in Austria. The Premonstratensians produced a fine abbey which passed into private hands following the Dissolution in the 1530s. In 1929 the complex was purchased by Torquay Corporation and it now serves as a public art gallery having works by Turner, Etty and Holman Hunt. Quite substantial remains are fringed by colourful gardens including the 12th century Chapter House Entrance, a splendid gatehouse dating to the 14th century and a guest house built at the same time. In some ways the most exciting remains of the old abbey is what has become known as the Spanish Barn although it was originally the monks' storehouse. The reason for the change of name was because following the defeat of the Armada, 400 Spanish prisoners were kept in the barn. The present building known as Torre Abbey was the home of the Cavy family and dates mainly to the 17th and 18th century.

Whilst picnicking in the gardens we got into conversation with a gentleman in his 90s who told us of his memories of the nearby village of Kingskerswell where each May Day there was a session of maypole dancing in front of the church of St. Mary. After this we drove to the church and looked at the magnificent effigy of the 14th century Knight, Sir John Dinham shown in full armour and with his head resting on an angel. Behind all successful men there is said to be a successful woman, but in the life of Sir John there were two and both the wives of the Knight in armour are depicted in his memorial.

From Kingkerswell we returned to Torquay via Babbacombe quite rightly famous for its model village which is open every day from Easter to the end of October from 9 am to 10 pm and during the darker months from 9 am to dusk. It is a fascinating view of the old English countryside in miniature including thatched cottages, farms, railways with locomotives passing over bridges, lakes and waterfalls all landscaped using dwarf conifers. There is even a model of a modern town, the whole being a photographer's delight. Although Cockington Forge is a real village we can never resist comparing it to Babbacombe because it is so commercialised these days that it does not feel to be lived in by real people. Nobody can, however, deny that its tangle of colourful thatched buildings is as fine a view as every graced a postcard. The 14th century forge is now a shop like most of the other old buildings with the whole settlement fringed by rather ugly modern houses.

Apart from its model village Babbacombe beach is worth a visit in its own right as it was a resort favoured by Royalty long before Torquay began to dominate. It was the haunt of smugglers right up to 1853 when the customs' officers confiscated no fewer than 153 casks of spirits.

On the opposite side of the Bay is Oddicombe which is dominated by contrasting cliffs of red sandstone and pale limestone. There is a cliff railway from the smooth clean sandy shore to the clifftop across which runs the South Devon coastal path.

Torquay itself has plenty of real history, being initiated by the monks of Torre Abbey. They built a new quay on the north side of Tor Bay but prior to this there had been a small hamlet called Tormohun lying snug beneath a Tor of the same name.

Cockington Forge on a quiet winter's morning. It is far busier in the summer.

This remained the broad pattern until the early years of the 19th century when the south facing slopes between Tormohun and Tor Bay sprouted increasing numbers of mostly elegant mansions. The fishermens' cottages around the monks' quay were swamped, especially following the arrival of a branch of the railway from Newton Abbot in 1848. By 1850 Torquay was seeking to increase its share of the tourist trade by claiming the title 'the Queen of Watering Places'. This glorious Victorian Age is described in the 'Bygones' Museum in Fore Street at St. Marygate on the outskirts of Torquay. It is housed in an old cinema and has a much larger interior than you may think. It opens every day of the year from 10 am to 5 pm but from June to September Bygones remains open until 10 pm. There is plenty of parking and there is so much to see here that to rush around would be a waste of money and the opportunity to experience the elegance of a long gone age. There is a real Victorian street which has been rebuilt in all detail and included is a pub and a blacksmith's forge which was just as essential in its day as a petrol station is today. There is an exhibition of railways both real and model whilst the children are provided with miniature fantasylands. Grandad is not forgotten either for here is one of the best collections of militaria to be found in Devon. There is a good coffee bar and a souvenir shop. The settlement of St. Marychurch is obviously named after the church which only dates to 1861 although it contains a

Saxon font supporting its claim of being the oldest Christian settlement in Devon. After our visit to 'Bygones' we had a picnic lunch on the Marine Drive and we were treated to a free exhibition of nostalgia as a fully rigged sailing ship eased her way slowly round the point towards Paignton.

Before leaving Torquay for Paignton there are a number of attractions which should not be missed including wandering among the palm trees to the harbour which combine to produce of genuine feel of the Mediterranean and the local boast of being the English Riviera is not an exaggeration. There are thousands of pleasure craft of all shapes, sizes and prices and particularly in the summer there is a wide range of day trips some of which are cruises reaching as far as the Channel Islands. There are several beaches around Torquay where coastal wildlife can be studied and for those who want to identify their observations a visit to the aquarium will be helpful, but perhaps this is one of the many attractions which should be left for a wet day. Another is the English Riviera Leisure Centre near Torre Abbey.

Paignton is quite rightly proud of having one of the best zoos in the country opened in 1923, being situated on Totnes Road and open from 10 am every day of the year except Christmas Day. Not only is it in our view one of the best zoos but it is also one of the largest and on display are more than 300 species of animal in 75 acres (30 hectares) of well manicured botanical gardens through which runs a miniature railway. The zoo has recently constructed a rhino house which proves that the authorities have their eye firmly set on the fact that the welfare of the animals comes first and conservation is high on the agenda. There are also 25 acres (10 hectares) of native woodland with a nature trail running through it. There are good facilities for the disabled and extensive picnic areas, a snack bar and restaurant and a family activity centre. Before exploring the town many visitors prefer to enjoy a trip on one of Britain's best preserved and most scenic steam railways. Services run from March to November with Santa Special Services running in December. The Paignton and Dartmouth Steam Railway is seven miles of the best the old Great Western had to offer and advertises itself as the 'Nation's Holiday Line'. One of our vivid memories of South Devon was

Brixham harbour with the replica of the Golden Hind in the background.

on a warm gentle June day when we joined the Boat Train Circular. This leaves Paignton for Kingswear via Goodrington and Churston. The Round Robin ticket includes a ferry trip across to Dartmouth and then a cruise up the river to Totnes. The return journey to Paignton is by bus. This journey through glorious and varied scenery avoids parking problems and there are souvenir shops and cafes at Paignton and Kingswear whilst there are buffet facilities on the river cruisers.

Paignton was a small settlement from Saxon times but followed the usual pattern for this area by expanding rapidly following the arrival of the railway in this case in December 1859. By the time of the Norman Conquest Paignton belonged to the Bishop of Exeter and the area around the church developed as, and is still, the centre of the settlement but is now encircled by the pleasant 16th and 17th century cottages on Church Street and Kirkham Street. At this time the area was known as Paignton Well. Parts of St. John's church is obviously of Norman origin as the west door clearly illustrates and nearby are the ruins of the old palace of the Bishop of Exeter of which one solid tower remains. Although this is called Coverdale Tower there does not seem to be any evidence to support the legend that the first man to translate the Bible into English spent time in Paignton. Kirkham House in Mill Lane also dates to the 15th century and there is some debate regarding its function, which may have been the home of a rich merchant or perhaps used

The developing Brixham marina.

as a lodging for the high ranking servants of the Bishop. The latter would seem to be the more likely. This building almost fell down but since 1960 it has been restored, furnished in the manner of the period and is open to the public.

Almost in the centre of the town is a more modern building, but one with an interesting tale to tell as Oldway Mansion was constructed in 1874 for the man who made his fortune from sewing machines – Isaac Singer. His son was true to his Christian name of Paris and extended the house until it had 115 rooms of breathtaking elegance including wonderful plaster ceilings and an attempt to duplicate the Hall of Mirrors at Versailles. The gardens are also beautiful, the building being used as the Council Offices but with a number of rooms and the gardens open to the public.

Paignton has two further aspects left to discover – its harbour and its beach, or rather beaches, because it has two. Although quite small the harbour, built in 1838 and sheltered by Roundham Head, is busy with fishermen and crabs and lobsters can be bought here. Just writing about them sets our taste buds running. Pleasure trips operate from the harbour and the aquarium is also worth an extended visit. Paignton beaches are separated by Redcliffe headland and there is also a pier, a structure which is something of a rarity in the West Country. The local rowing club use the arches of the pier to practice

Brixham trawlers were a common sight up to the 1920's. Their graceful lines would do justice to a pleasure craft.

their sprint starts. All the beaches in the area are clean and safe for bathing and at Goodrington is Quaywest which is the largest water theme park in the country and entry is through the beach and is free. All that has to be paid for are the rides and there is car parking space for nearly 2000 cars.

Those, like us we must admit, who prefer more peaceful and historic places then Brixham is the complete answer. We have spent many years studying the history of the maritime heritage of Britain with emphasis on fishing and the most famous vessel of all is the Brixham Trawler. In its day this was one of the most impressive sailing vessels ever built and so efficient were they that Brixham in the 18th century was the most profitable fishing

Maypole dancing was once a feature of many Devon villages around 1900. Here is the ceremony of Kingkerswell near Torquay.

port in Britain. It held this position until the shipbuilders of Fleetwood, Hull and Lowestoft learned to construct these 75 foot (23 metre) masters of the sea. A few still remain in the area and are a joy to see.

Fishing is still the mainstay of Brixham's fortunes and the yachts and pleasure boats have to weave in and out of the modern trawlers, and the fleet is still important. Fishing fleets should not just be watched, they should be taken advantage of and we love to wander among the nets, floats and fish boxes, smell the brine, fish and diesel and taste the seafood and the fresh succulent fish. Once again those on self-catering holidays have the advantage of being able to choose and cook their own food.

However many seaside holiday attractions there are in the area it is impossible to escape from the commercial maritime aspects at Brixham. Here is the base for the coastguard, the Life Boat and the Royal Mission to Deep Sea Fishermen. The Harbourmaster always goes home tired after a hard day's work organising a vast number and variety of vessels busy about their business. Tourists are offered a variety of local pleasure trips

The Razorbill is a common breeding bird on the cliffs around Tor Bay.

but you can even enjoy a day fishing for sharks. Lying snugly in the inner harbour is a replica of Sir Francis Drake's ship the *Golden Hind* which was adapted from an old trawler and it is open to the public. Below decks there are displays describing various aspects of maritime history. If this is a bit of contrived history then Brixham has a genuine claim to a place in British national as well as local history. In 1688 William of Orange landed at Brixham at the head of an army and determined to fight to realise his own and Mary's claim to the throne. In the event his claim was accepted without a fight as we have seen at Newton Abbot and a bond was established with Holland which has survived for around 300 years. In July 1988 Queen

Elizabeth II and the present Prince of Orange met at Brixham with great ceremony to re-create the landing and in 1989 the first stage of the new boating marina, which has berths for 500 yachts and is called Prince William Quay, was completed.

There are wonderful views from Berry Head Country Park which has survived a real battering at the hands of limestone quarrymen. The area has been settled at least since the Iron Age when a fort was built overlooking the Bay. In the late 18th and early 19th century, Britain was at war with France and many forts were built as part of a defensive link. Few were better sited than the one on Berry Head, built in 1802, and from which Portland Bill can be seen on a good day, a distance of 46 miles as the seabird flies. The cliffs here have nesting auks including razorbill and guillemot plus fulmar and kittiwake. Leaflets describing the wildlife can be purchased at a cafe situated in the Napoleonic fort. Obviously this is the ideal place for a lighthouse and it has been said that Berry Head has the highest and the lowest lighthouse in Britain even though there is only one structure. The building is only 15 feet (4.6 metres) tall but what does it need height for when it stands on top of a 200 foot (61 metre) cliff.

We love exploring cities but don't like sleeping in them. Our favourite route into Plymouth is to set off early in the morning from Brixham to arrive in the city for breakfast with the car parked safely for the day, and to leave in the mid-evening after dinner when the traffic has had time to clear. This route and Plymouth itself are the subject of the final chapter.

CHAPTER 8

Around Plymouth

Plymouth is a large city but it does not have a cathedral as it has no Bishop, its religious life being governed from Exeter where we began our journey of discovery. Since it was devastated by bombing Plymouth has risen like a Phoenix from the ashes, and there is so much to see that it is difficult to know where to start to describe the development in and around the estuaries of three rivers the Yealm, the Plym and the Tamar. A happy accident provided us with what turned out to be the best way to discover Plymouth. We were asked to take part in a television series by T.V.S. who based us in a large hotel overlooking Plymouth Hoe and as we arrived by train a day before the shoot we had time to explore the city on foot. As the programme had a natural history base and we are both naturalists the obvious place to start was at the world famous marine aquarium sheltered beneath the massive walls of the Citadel. Although the aquarium is open to the public it has never ceased to be a working marine laboratory and is even more interesting because of this. This is no mere zoo but is continuing to make massive contributions to world conservation. It began in 1888 to co-ordinate the work of the Marine Biological Association of the United Kingdom founded four years previously. It now has its own research vessels and some of their catches are on display in the tanks. This means that exhibitions are constantly changing and concentrate heavily, but not exclusively, on species found in British waters.

The Royal Citadel is a very solid reminder of old Plymouth and was built in 1666, although its impressive baroque-style gateway was not complete until 1670. The Citadel is now the home base of No 29 Commando Royal Artillery and there is obviously restricted access to the building but there are regular guided tours and the route includes the Governor's House and the Royal Chapel dedicated to St. Katherine. Charles II ordered the construction of the Citadel in the 1660s because he feared the people of Plymouth who had been such firm supporters of

Parliament when Cromwell's forces defeated those of his father. They then had Charles I executed in 1649 at the end of the Civil War. The citadel staffed with his best and most loyal officers who were the restored King's insurance policy.

There is so much history concerned with Plymouth that for years it cried out for an all-embracing museum and in the late 1980s and early 1990s this was provided by the construction of Plymouth Dome, already regarded as one of the best museum complexes in Europe and which is open each day except Christmas Day from 10 am and in the season it remains open until what the management calls 'late'. Situated on the Hoe, the building has been so well planned that it does not interfere with the magnificent view out to sea. There is good access for the disabled and special rates for parties and we feel half a day at least should be allowed within the complex and is an ideal venue if the weather is wet. Touring the Dome is like walking through the history of Plymouth including the gun deck of a typical Elizabethan galleon, experiencing the atmosphere aboard the Pilgrim Fathers' Mayflower and the important rôle played by Plymouth during the Civil War. The fear created by the 'press gangs' in supplying the navy with ratings and what it was like to be living in the area during the Blitz when the German Luftwaffe inflicted so much death and destruction are also graphically explained. These are not static displays but life-sized cameos and scenes including real actors. Even the sounds and smells of the periods have been recreated. Small wonder that the Dome is winning an increasing number of awards and here computers have been brought into service as a back-up and enhancing system accompanying the historical scenes. Here it is possible to get to know Plymouth and after a rest in the restaurant set off with a list of places to explore made in the comfort of the Dome.

Plymouth Sound is the largest of the rias on the south west peninsula and is one of the world's finest deepwater anchorages, and to us, who may well be biased, a rival to Valetta's Grand Harbour on Malta where we have also spent many happy hours just watching the ships. Such a vast expanse could hardly have developed into a single city without smaller settlements developing along its inlets and three were more important than the other hamlets. Davenport on the Tamar

The Barbican, Plymouth's earliest harbour.

PILGRIMS
WHO SAILED FROM HERE, THE BARBICAN PLYMOUTH, IN 1620 IN THE MAYFLOWER 180 TONS. CHRISTOPHER JONES, MASTER

JOHN ALDEN, COOPER, HARWICH - THE FIRST TO STEP ASHORE
JOHN CARVER, DONCASTER, MERCHANT
KATHERINE CARVER, HIS WIFE
JOHN HOWLAND, MAN SERVANT, LONDON
ROGER WILDER, MAN SERVANT
DESRE MINTER - WILLIAM LATHAM, SERVANT BOY
JASPER MORE, SERVANT BOY - A MAID SERVANT
WILLIAM BREWSTER, SCROOBY, NOTTS
MARY BREWSTER, HIS WIFE
LOVE BREWSTER, HIS SON
WRASLING BREWSTER, HIS SON
RICHARD MORE, SERVANT BOY
— MORE, BROTHER OF RICHARD
EDWARD WINSLOW, DROITWICH, PRINTER
ELIZABETH WINSLOW, HIS WIFE
GEORGE SOWLE, MANSERVANT - ELIAS STORY, MANSERVANT
ELLEN MORE, SERVANT GIRL, SISTER OF RICHARD
WILLIAM BRADFORD, YORKS, FUSTIAN MAKER - DOROTHY HIS WIFE
ISAAC ALLERTON, LONDON, TAILOR - MARY ALLERTON, HIS WIFE
BARTHOLOMEW ALLERTON, HIS SON
REMEMBER AND MARY ALLERTON, HIS DAUGHTERS
JOHN HOOKE, SERVANT BOY
SAMUELL FULLER, SAIL MAKER, SHIPS PHYSITION AND CHIRURGEON
WILLIAM BUTTER, HIS SERVANT OF AUSTERFIELD, DIED ON VOYAGE
JOHN CRAKSTON OF COLCHESTER AND HIS SON JOHN
CAPTAIN MYLES STANDISH, SOLDIER, CHORLEY, LANCASHIRE
ROSE STANDISH, HIS WIFE
CHRISTOPHER MARTIN, GREAT BURSTEAD, ESSEX
— MARTIN, HIS WIFE
SALAMON PROWER AND JOHN LANGEMORE, HIS SERVANTS
WILLIAM MULLINES, SHOPKEEPER, DORKING SURREY
— MULLINES, HIS WIFE
JOSEPH MULLINES, HIS SON
PRISCILLA MULLINES, HIS DAUGHTER
ROBART CARTER, HIS SERVANT
WILLIAM WHITE, WOOL CARDER, AND SUSANA HIS WIFE
RESOLVED WHITE, HIS SON AND PEREGRIENE, SON, BORN ON BOARD
WILLIAM HOLBECK, HIS SERVANT
EDWARD THOMSON, HIS SERVANT
STEVEN HOPKINS, WOTTON UNDER EDGE, GLOUCESTER
ELIZABETH HOPKINS, HIS WIFE
GILES HOPKINS, HIS SON - CONSTANTA HOPKINS, HIS DAUGHTER
DAMARIS HOPKINS, HIS DAUGHTER AND OCEANUS, BORN ON VOYAGE
EDWARD DOTY AND EDWARD LITSTER, HIS SERVANTS
RICHARD WARREN, MERCHANT LONDON
JOHN BILLINTON, LONDON, ELEN BILLINTON, HIS WIFE
JOHN BILLINTON, HIS SON, FRANCIS BILLINTON, HIS SON
EDWARD TILLIE, CLOTH MAKER OF LONDON
ANN TILLIE, HIS WIFE
HENERY SAMSON, THEIR COSSEN, A CHILD
HUMILITY COOPER, THEIR COSSEN, A CHILD
JOHN TILLIE, SILK WORKER OF LONDON
BRIDGET TILLIE, HIS WIFE
ELIZABETH TILLIE, HIS DAUGHTER
FRANCIS COOKE, WOOL COMBER OF BLYTH, JOHN COOKE, HIS SON
THOMAS ROGERS, CAMLET MERCHANT, JOSEPH ROGERS, HIS SON
THOMAS TINKER, WOOD SAWYER
— TINKER, HIS WIFE AND — HIS SON
JOHN RIGDALE, LONDON, ALIC RIGDALE, HIS WIFE
JAMES CHILTON, CANTERBURY, TAILOR
— CHILTON, HIS WIFE, MARY CHILTON, HIS DAUGHTER
EDWARD FULLER, REDENHALL, NORFOLK
— FULLER, HIS WIFE, SAMUELL FULLER, HIS SON
JOHN TURNER, MERCHANT AND HIS TWO SONS
FRANCIS EATON, BRISTOL, CARPENTER
SARAH EATON, HIS WIFE, SAMUEL EATON, HIS SON
MOYSES FLETCHER, SMITH, SANDWICH
JOHN GOODMAN, LINEN WEAVER
THOMAS WILLIAMS, YARMOUTH, NORFOLK
DIGERIE PRIEST, LONDON, HATTER, EDMOND MARGESON
PETER BROWNE, GREAT BURSTEAD, ESSEX
RICHARD BUTTERIGE, RICHARD CLARKE
RICHARD GARDENAR, HARWICH, GILBART WINSLOW
JOHN ALLERTON, MARINER, THOMAS ENLISH, MARINER
WILLIAM TREVORE, SAILOR, ELY, SAILOR

The Pilgrim Fathers' plaque on the Barbican.

which marks the boundary with Cornwall was furthest to the west, with Stonehouse in the middle and Plymouth to the east literally being at the mouth of the River Plym. The population is now more than 300,000, and its prime position in the annals of the British Navy is because South Devon produced most of England's finest seamen during the 16th century including Drake, Raleigh, Hawkins and Gilbert. There was no conscious effort to recognise Plymouth as the official base of the navy until 1689 when William of Orange gave orders to build a Royal Dockyard on the marshland around Davenport which at that time was about a mile to the west of Plymouth. The expanding strength of the navy soon rushed into this geographical vacuum.

Although the blitz destroyed many fine old buildings enough remain to give a feeling of the Elizabethan city especially in the area of the Barbican. It was from here in 1620 that the Pilgrim Fathers finally set sail for the New World, and to which the Tolpuddle Martyrs returned from exile to their old houses in 1838 but no doubt filled with trepidation. The Barbican is a surprisingly small harbour overlooked by wonderful buildings and used by fishing and pleasure vessels all reflected in the sheltered waters. Swans sail majestically around begging food from the visitors.

The best way to explore the Sound and the city is to take one or more of a choice of four cruises from the Mayflower Steps at the Barbican. Our favourite is a one hour trip taking in the dockyard and warships with good views of the Hoe and Drake's Island. Dominating the Hoe is Smeaton's Tower brightly painted in red and white and stands as proud today as it did when it stood guard 14 miles out to sea over the Eddystone rocks in the 18th century. In 1882 Smeaton's light was replaced by a larger lighthouse being dismantled stone by stone and erected on the Hoe, to become Plymouth's most famous landmark.

Nearby is a statue of Drake who is said to have played his famous game of bowls here whilst waiting for the wind and tide to change and allow the fleet to sail and tackle the Spanish fleet. The Hoe itself is not as ancient as the Barbican and is a breakwater of about one mile in length, designed by John Rennie. Completed in 1840 it took 28 years to build from

The Smeaton Lighthouse on Plymouth Hoe.

limestone and granite blocks dovetailed together. Rennie also designed the naval supply centre known as the Royal William Victualling Yard built between 1826 and 1835. It is situated at Stonehouse about a mile west of the Hoe but is not open to the public, although its impressive facade can be seen from the pleasure cruiser. William IV was not a very impressive or well liked man and nobody was displeased when he was succeeded by his niece Victoria. He was, however, known as the Sailor King and this yard is a tribute to him with six of its fifteen acres reclaimed from the sea.

Drake's Island was once dedicated to St. Nicholas but was named after Sir Francis following his return from circumnavigating the world in 1580. A fort was constructed in the 15th century but Drake was instrumental in extending the defensive potential of the island and it is said that the mariner himself undertook the first period of guard duty himself. After a period of service as an adventure centre the island is now back to a period of peace and quiet under the control of the Crown.

On returning to the Barbican there are other museums which should be visited but time should always be allowed to explore the antique shops, admire the work of the resident artists, watch the boats here and at the nearby Sutton Pool, or sample one of the many restaurants in the area. If you preface your meal with a gin and tonic then Plymouth has yet another treat in store for you. The Plymouth Dry Gin Distillery adjoining and contemporary with the old Blackfriars monastery mostly long demolished. It is on Southside Street near the Barbican. It opens from 10.30 am to 4 pm Monday to Saturday and from Easter to the end of September, although there is an attached bar which does a roaring trade with locals as well as visitors. The building was once the refectory of the monastery but after the Reformation was the mansion of Sir Joh Hele and later after a period as a wine coopery became a gin distillery in 1793 and has turned out the wonderful stuff ever since. Gin is a spirit distilled from grain or malt and the guided tour explains how the stills work, points out the spirit safes and how such plants as juniper are used to flavour Plymouth Dry Gin.

If this whets your appetite for museums then Plymouth has three of particular note, the City Museum and Art Gallery entry to which is free, the Merchant's House and Elizabethan House museums to which a small entry fee is charged. All three have the same opening times from Tuesday to Saturday from 10 am to 5.30 pm and on Sundays from 2 pm to 5 pm. This is the case throughout the year and they also open on summer Bank Holidays. This trio should not be looked upon as rivals to the new Dome but each as an extra dimension to all who wish to discover the 'soul' of Plymouth. It developed from a 12th century huddle of fishermens' cottages around Sutton Pool and not much different from those at Beesands. Both the Merchant's House and the Elizabethan House are buildings which are period pieces in their own right even if they contained nothing of interest within which is far from the case. The Merchant's House on St. Andrew's Street was the home of William Parker, an Elizabethan gentleman, who was mayor of Plymouth and had his residence constructed at great expense. The furnishings and exhibits tell the story of Elizabethan England but there is also a mock-up of an old pharmacy which proves what people were prepared to eat and drink in the belief that they would feel better. The timber-framed dwellings with overhanging jetties have changed little since

The new Plymouth Dome on the Hoe.

Drake's time and he may well have supped with the owner of what is now the Elizabethan House Museum on New Street. This once belonged to a sea-captain and its furnishings are genuine pieces of the period. It is even said to have a resident ghost. The City Museum at Drake's Circus houses a display of local natural history and also of the minerals of Cornwall which were exported through Plymouth. There is also a good collection of fine porcelain made locally and the art gallery is also impressive as is the transparent bee hive, which enables the hard working insects to be closely observed. The exhibition of pre-historic Dartmoor is of particular relevance to students of Devon in general rather than Plymouth in particular.

Living history can also be enjoyed, not only around the Barbican but also around Sutton Pool which still has a thriving fish market. Although Dartmoor tin was also exported via the Pool it was not the first choice but the pollution and debris had affected the Plym so badly that it was no longer a reliable harbour. The City has also kept well in tune with the 1990s with the opening of Plymouth Pavilions which combines an exhibition, entertainment and conference centre with a leisure pool, ice rink and restaurants all under one roof, thus providing holiday entertainment even when it is raining. The Theatre Royal in the heart of the city is one of Britain's major provincial theatres. Apart from performances it opens to the public from 10 am each day except Sunday and there is a theatre shop, craft shop, Pizza and Pasta Catering plus the up-market Broadway restaurant, and two bars.

As mentioned earlier Plymouth is a city lacking a cathedral and both of its interesting churches failed to survive the blitz. Only the shell of the Charles church which was built in 1664 remains. This is said to be the only church built in Devon in the 17th century and its ruin now stands in the middle of a road roundabout and left as a gaunt memorial to the 1,172 people of the city who were killed by German bombs. The parish church of St. Andrew was also bombed and although restored its character was blasted out of it. Fortunately the 15th century tower escaped, and not all the Luftwaffe's attentions were destructive because the damage exposed some wall paintings which although quite crude illustrate the exploits of Sir Francis Drake. A more modern tribute to Drake is the 20th century stained glass window by John Piper. Near the church is the 15th century Prysten or Priests' House said to be the oldest building in the city and built for the monks of Plympton Priory. The house opens between 10 am and 4 pm between April and October and there is a small entry fee. Inside is a model of Plymouth as it was in 1620 and an exhibition of tapestry making. Plympton is one of several areas outside Plymouth which is well worth discovering along with Yealmpton and Sparkwell.

There are actually two Plymptons – Plympton St. Mary and Plympton St. Maurice built around the lands and buildings of the Priory and initially this area was of far more importance than the area around Sutton Pool. Plympton is thus the place to discover the region's most impressive churches. The Augustinian Priory was founded in 1121 with a delightful church constructed on its site with its pinnacled tower being a prominent landmark for miles around. Within are wall memorials to the Parker family who then lived at Boringdon House to the north of the church. Later they moved to Saltram, a magnificent 18th century house near Plymstock. The second Plympton has a church dedicated to St. Thomas and where Samuel Reynolds was rector. He is famous only as the father of the famous portrait painter Sir Joshua Reynolds. Why should the church of St. Thomas be in the village of St. Maurice? There was once a 14th century Chantry chapel here dedicated to St. Maurice. All traces of this have gone but there is just a trace of a Norman castle and standing on a raised hump is the shape of a circular Norman keep. From here there are excellent views. Before leaving Plympton St. Maurice the old Grammar school should be seen for two reasons – its elegant arcade of Tudor pillars and because it was here that Joshua Reynolds began his education as his father combined the duties of headmaster with his rôle as Rector of the church. Plympton St Maurice was also once an important stannary town and the 17th century Guildhall has been restored and is open to visitors.

Saltram House is just off the A38 about two miles west of Plympton. There was certainly a house on the site in Tudor times and although the Parkers bought the house in 1712 they did not take up permanent residence until 1743 when John Parker set about transforming Saltram, and this was complete by 1750. In 1788 John Parker II was the owner and although he was only a country squire he did have influential friends including Sir Joshua Reynolds, and the good taste to employ Robert Adam to put his skills to use in the house. The squire was also a good judge of horse flesh and even bred a Derby winner called Saltram. The name derives from the fact that this area was once an important salt producing area using salt pans in the Plym estuary. Now one of Devon's largest country houses Saltram is famous for its Adam interiors and its Reynold's paintings. The house is said to have the finest collection of paintings to be found in Devon and a feature of the gardens is an orangery. There are woodlands running down to the river. It is open daily from Easter to the end of October except Friday and Saturday from 12.30 pm to 6 pm for the house but the garden is open from 11 am to 6 pm (5 pm in October). There is a licenced restaurant in the house and exhibitions and shop in the stables. For those who enjoy walking, a trip to Saltram House should be followed by a picnic lunch and an exploration of the Plym Bridge trail established by the National Trust. There is a large car park and the wooded walk following the line of a disused railway is always open. In spring the damp woodlands hang heavy with the smell of wild garlic, but they are of interest throughout the year.

The National Shire Horse Centre near Plymouth is the finest museum of its type in Britain.

Within an easy drive of Plymouth is Yealmpton which has two tourist traps of its own. These are Kitley Caves and the National Shire Horse Centre. The Caves are open during Easter and then from May to the end of October between 10 am and 5 pm. There are extensive underground caverns beautifully lit and once the refuge of Stone Age man, mammoths, hyenas and bears all of which is explained in an imaginatively set out Interpretation Centre. This also includes an explanation of the local limekilns and the part their products played in the local economy. Obviously the underground system is an ideal wet weather attraction but on a good day there are woodland and riverside walks with areas laid out for picnics. Energetic children are provided with an adventure playground and there is plenty of parking, cafes and a gift and souvenir shop specialising in crystals and minerals.

The National Shire Horse Centre is open throughout the year from 10 am to 5 pm except the period 23 to 26 December and there is a parade of the gentle giants at 11.30 am, 2.30 pm and 4.15 pm. If there was nothing here but horses the centre would be excellent value but there is also a falconry centre organising regular flights at 1 pm and 3 pm, a butterfly house, blacksmith's forge, a craft centre with a saddler and a glass engraver. Here we were introduced to *King*, a Shire horse standing 19.2 hands at the shoulder and weighing over 1,000 kilos. A more gentle giant it would be impossible to find. One hand is equal to 4 inches and thus he is 6 feet 6 inches (1.9 metres) plus his massive

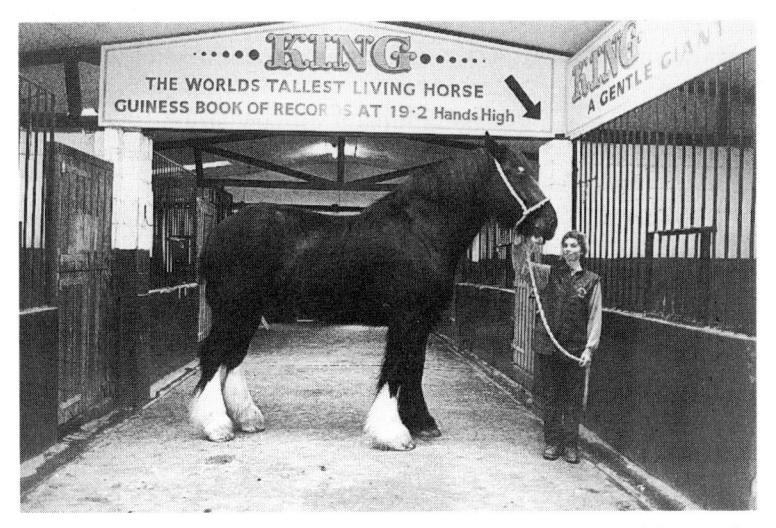

King of the Horses – the largest in the world at his stables at the National Shire Horse Museum.

neck and head. He also demands King size shoes with his farrier having to hammer away at a 19 inch (47 cms) ring of steel! The Guiness Book of Records accepts that here is the World's Tallest Horse. There is a pets' area, and unusually dogs are welcome here which is typical of one of the friendliest working museums we have ever encountered. There is a restaurant and a gift shop, with the whole complex providing a full and enjoyable day whatever the weather. On a fine day there is a walk down to the River Yealm via the centre's farm. Shire horses are becoming ever rarer these days and what a joy it is to see so many of the beasts in the full flush of health, coats gleaming and brasses shining. Each day they pull cart loads of visitors around the centre and appear to love every minute of it.

Whilst the Shire Horses at Yealmpton have no rivals to compete for visitors the falcons do as the Dartmoor Wildlife Park and West Country Falconry Centre at Sparkwell also has flying displays. The Centre is open on every day of the year from 10 am until dusk. Set in more than 30 acres of delightful countryside there are more than 150 species of mammals including big cats, birds, especially owls and falcons, plus a variety of reptiles. There is plenty of free parking, picnic site, restaurant and a bar, a souvenir shop and donkey rides for the children.

The Plym was once the dominant estuary around Plymouth but its supremacy has long been taken over by the Tamar a river which forms a natural border between Devon and Cornwall with Plymouth on one side and Saltash on the other. This is one of the most attractive routes into Cornwall yet another of England's beautiful counties.

Further Reading

Booker, F. (1983) *Morwellham Quay – in the Tamar Valley* (Jarrold)
Born, Anne (1983) *South Devon, Combe, Tor and Seascape* (Gollanez)
Bound, T. (1991) *The A to Z of Dartmoor Tors* (Obelisk Publications)
Breton, H. (1911) *Beautiful Dartmoor* (Reprinted by Forest Publishing 1990)
Burrows, Roger (1971) *The Naturalist in Devon and Cornwall* (David and Charles)
Clew, K. R. (1984) *The Exeter Canal* (Phillimore)
Crossings (1912) *Guide to Dartmoor* (Reprinted by the Penninsula Press 1990)
Crossings (1902) *The Ancient Stone Crosses of Dartmoor* (1987 Edition by Devon Books)
Freethy, Ron (1981) *The Naturalists' Guide to the British Coastline* (David and Charles)
Freethy, Ron (1986) *British Ferns in their Habitats* (Crowood Press)
Freethy, Ron (1986, 1992) *Woodlands – a Naturalist's Guide* (Bell and Hyman, Collins)
Hoskins, W. G. (1960) *Two Thousand Years in Exeter* (Phillimore)
Lawrence, R. (1991) *The Exe a river of Wildlife* (Ex-Libris Press)
Little, B. (1983) *Portrait of Exeter* (Hale)
Lowther, K. E. and Hammond, R. J. N. (1979) *Ward Lock Red Guide to Dartmoor* (Ward Lock)
Palmer, J. (1990) *The Dartmoor Pony – A History of the Breed* (Devon Press)
Pilkington, P. (1989) *Ashburton The Dartmoor Town* (Devon Books)
Stainer, P. (1988) *Devon* (Shire Publications)
Stuart, E. (1991) *Lost Landscapes of Plymouth* (Alan Sutton)
Toulson, Shirley (1991) *The Companion Guide to Devon* (Harper Collins)

Index

A-La-Ronde 137–139
Alvington 97
Ashburn, river, 25
Ashburton 26–28, 78
Axmouth 108, 115, 116
Axminster 108, 109–111, 115

Babbacombe 147, 151–152
Becky Falls 57–58
Beer 14, 115, 117–119
Beesands 104, 105
Belstone 55
Berry Head 8, 159
Berry Pomeroy Castle 86–87
Bicton Park 133
Blachford Park 37
Black Tor Beare 7
Bolt Head 107
Bovey Tracey 57–60
Bowerman's Nose 58
Bowhill 25
Branscombe 108, 115, 120–121
Bridford 52–64
Brixham 108, 141, 154, 155, 166–169
Buckfast Abbey 33–34, 97
Buckfastleigh 26, 29–34
Buckland Abbey 44–46
Buckland-on-the-Moor 28, 29
Budleigh Salterton 129–136
Burrator reservoir 45

Cadhay 129
Canonteign Country Park 62–64
Castle Drogo 65
Cattedown 5
Chagford 9, 57, 62, 66–70, 78
Chillington 97
Christow 62
Chudleigh 24–25
Cockington Forge 152
Cornwood 37
Cotehele Quay 43–44
Crapstone 44
Crocken Tor 78

Croyle 109
Cullompton 108–109

Dart Bridge 26
Dartington 87–88
Dartmeet 79
Dartmouth 80, 86, 87, 89–97
Dart River Country Park 28–29
Dartmoor Prison *see* Princetown
Dawlish 108, 140, 141–143
Dean Prior 34–36
Dittisham Prehistoric settlement 87, 88–89
Dunsford 64

Ermington 37–38
Erne river 36, 37
Exeter 8, 9, 11ff, 26
Exmoor 3
Exmouth 136–140

Fardel Manor 37
Farway Country Park 113–115
Fanworthy Forest 70–71
Fingle Bridge 64–66
Furzeleigh Woods 57

Gidleigh 71
Greator Rocks 58
Grimspound 5, 7, 76 77
Gunnislake 43–44

Hallsands 104–105
Harford 37–38
Hawkesdown Hill 115–116
Haytor 60
Hemyock Castle 113–114
Holne 28, 29
Holne Chase Camp 29
Honiton 108, 111–112
Hound Tor 58

Ivybridge 26, 36–37, 38

174

Kennick reservoir 58
Kentisbeare 109
Kents Cavern 5, 31, 149–150
Kinkerswell 157
Kingsbridge 36, 80, 97–100
Kingswear 96–97
Kitley Caves 170

Ladram Bay 123, 124
Lew river 53
Lustleigh 58–59
Lydford Gorge 46–48

Malborough 80
Manaton 58
Mary Tavy 46
Merrivale 10
Modbury 80
Moretonhampstead 57, 61–63, 64
Morwellham Quay 39, 40, 41–43

Newton Abbot 144–147
Northlew 55, 56
North Tawton 55, 56

Okehampton 26, 51–55
Okement West river 51
Oreston 5
Otterton Mill 112, 131–136
Ottery St Mary 14, 108, 125–136

Paignton 141, 153–156
Piles Copse 7
Plymouth 2, 3, 26, 36, 38, 97, 107, 140, 141, 159, 160ff
Plym river 160
Plymptons, the 9, 78, 168–169
Postbridge 57, 74–76
Powderham Castle 24–25
Prestonbury 8, 64
Princetown 5, 10, 57, 62, 76–78, 79

St Marychurch 152
Salcombe 106–107
Salcombe Regis 115, 121–122
Saltram House 169

Sampford Courteney 55–56
Sandy Bay 140
Seaton 108, 115, 116–117
Shaldon 144
Shaptor 57
Sheepstor 45
Shaugh Prior 3
Sidmouth 108, 122–123
Slapton 101–104
South Brent 6, 26, 36
South Hams 80ff
Stancombe 100–101
Star Cross 140
Start Bay 105
Stowford 37–38
Sticklepath Museum of Water Power 53–55
Stonehouse 5

Tamar River 80
Tavistock 9, 26, 38–42, 49–50, 78
Tavy river 44
Taw river 53
Teignmouth 143–144
Torbay 5, 7
Torquay 2, 5, 147–151
Torre Abbey 149–151
Torridge river 55
Totnes 9, 80–86
Tottiford reservoir 58
Trenchford reservoir 58
Two Bridges 78

Ugborough 37–38
Ugbrook House 25

Weburn river 28
Widecombe-in-the-Moor 57, 71–75
Wilton 110
Wistman's Wood 7

Yarner Wood 60–61
Yealm river 160
Yealmpton 5, 170–171
Yelverton 43–44